CW00551235

THE THIRD

MODEL RAILWAY JOURNAL
COMPENDIUM

Welcome to the Third Model Railway Journal Compendium, our occasional bumper bundle of all that is best in finescale modelling.

As many of you will already know, Compendium is a collection of articles in the MRJ tradition — only more so! The book format allows us to go into a little more detail where appropriate, as well as giving us the chance for some diversions away from the mainstream.

Our first-rate contributors in this issue include Gordon Gravett — taking us on a guided tour of his magnificent 7mm narrow gauge 'Aberynolwyn' layout — and Tim Shackleton, who has built a model of Gresley's bizarre 'Hush-Hush' 4–6–4 as well as an inspection saloon from the days when railway managers roamed the system in cigar-toting luxury. Dave Rowe is here to explain the building of one of those superb sailing barges from the famous 'Exebridge' diorama while Deryck Featherstone gets to grips with the intricate geometry devised to decorate Victorian engines and confuse us later generations. Look out too for the story of Captain Kelly, the rich and secretive blue-blood who played a surprisingly important part in the development of the hobby we know today.

That said, there is plenty of mainstream material to be found here. Stephen Williams, one of the team at Pendon Museum, builds a GWR 517 in 4mm/P4 and Martin Blackwell finds so many extra parts in a Finney GWR 'Dean Goods' kit that he manages to build two engines! And because GWR fans never get enough of what they fancy, there's a small Prairie kit-built as well. Still in Western territory, my favourite article is Mike Clark's matter-of-fact description of 'Hampstead Norris' — a layout doomed to the skip from the moment someone sawed it in half. For those who prefer something with a bit more logic, Wim Harthoorn shows you how to generate working model railway drawings on your home PC.

All this and more we present with warm good wishes from everyone at MRJ in this, our thirteenth year. It comes, above all else, with thanks for the friendship and support of our ever-growing band of readers throughout Britain and across the world.

Bob Barlow

CONTENTS

Edited by Bob Barlow and designed by Paul Karau
Printed by The Amadeus Press Ltd., Huddersfield

Published by Wild Swan Publications Ltd., 1-3 Hagbourne Road, Didcot, Oxon OX11 8DP
Tel: 01235 816478

ABERGYNOLWYN

The rain was so heavy on this particular morning there seemed no point in taking the camera out — the film would probably have got ruined, and besides, I had travelled on the Talyllyn Railway before, and in much better weather. A couple of colleagues and myself had gone to Wales for a few days holiday — in 1966 if my memory serves me right — to visit some of the narrow gauge lines, and today it was to be the Talyllyn.

The 2ft 3in gauge Tal-y-llyn Railway (the name was originally hyphenated) opened in 1865 to bring slate down from the quarries of Bryn Eglwys to a railhead at Towyn. The coastal resort of Towyn had not long been on the railway map as it was only two years earlier that the standard gauge line had been built along the coast from Aberdovey by the Aberystwyth & Welsh Coast Railway. By the time the Tal-y-llyn Railway had been built onto the wharf at Towyn the A&WCR had already been absorbed into the Cambrian. A passenger service was also introduced by the TR about 18 months later from the wharf at Towyn to Abergynolwyn, some six

GORDON GRAVETT describes his stunning 7mm diorama depicting a little slice of life on the Talyllyn Railway, now on permanent display at the TR's museum at Towyn:

miles up the line, but this village was in the bottom of the valley and the railway had by now climbed to about 242ft. Needless to say, there was a reasonable trek down from the station which was a mile or so short of the village.

A little further on, the mineral extension, as it was known, still climbing, passed high above Abergynolwyn; a winding house was built, straddling the track, for a rope-worked balanced incline down to the village. The railway continued to climb, around a narrow ledge cut into the hillside, towards a series of loop lines at the base of the Alltwyllt incline — this was the limit for locomotives as, from there on, a series of cable-worked inclines led up to the quarries. The preserved railway now runs as far as the foot of the Alltwyllt incline and Nant Gwernol station has been built on the site of the loops.

Abergynolwyn was not unique in having its own tramway, but such systems were hardly commonplace, and this one served both the industrial and domestic needs of the village. Materials could be brought in for various trades, coal could be delivered to the doors of the industries, and the tracks, which threaded their way along the backs of the cottages, could also discreetly remove night waste. The only rail connection with the outside world for the tramway was the balanced incline, but because this was not in line with the railway at the top, the rails from the village formed a crossroad inside the winding house. A loop around the back of the building and a wagon turntable gave access to the inclined tracks but, needless to say, this was for wagons only and the only motive power available at the bottom (in the village) was muscle power, either human or horse.

Dolgoch *on the rugged hillside above Abergynolwyn village.*

On the day of our visit we had planned to take the first train up from Towyn to the end of the line (as it was at the time) at Abergynolwyn, and then walk further up the old track towards the quarries, hoping that the outlook would get a bit brighter. The first stage of the walk took us along the overgrown tracks to the old winding house above Abergynolwyn village. This structure, although still standing, was in a dreadful state and was demolished fairly soon after. We still had a fair distance to go, so, despite the rain, we passed over the chance of shelter and marched on, battling through ever-thickening weeds and undergrowth that soaked us up to the knees. As I recall it, we trudged up a couple of the old inclines (Alltwyllt and Cantrybedd) and then took shelter in the remains of some old buildings at the top of Cantrybedd Incline, before calling it a day — a very wet and soggy one. Needless to say, the weather improved dramatically during the afternoon and, by the time our train had returned to Towyn, the sun was shining!

The memory of the old winding house had left an indelible mark somewhere within, as when the J.I.C. Boyd book *Talyllyn Railway* (Wild Swan) came out 20 years or more later, it was the chapter 'The Route from Wharf to Quarry' that I repeatedly turned. Here were some wonderful pictures of the section we had walked, but in pre-war days when the quarries were still in use, although even then they were in a very run-down and sorry state. If one photo stood out for me it was one of the loco *Taly-y-llyn* propelling a train of empty wagons through the structure on its way to the Alltwyllt incline. By this time, the large wooden lintel above the track, on the north face, had a frightful sag in it and, even then, drivers must have been holding their breath when the engine went through the building.

The winding house was very appealing from the modelling point of view, and initially I had thoughts of including it in some grand scheme based very loosely on the Tal-y-llyn Railway. I had already built the two TR locos, *Tal-y-llyn* and *Dolgoch* in 7mm scale, along with a selection of the railway's wagons (from Wrightlines kits), for a previous narrow gauge layout, so it made sense to build something else on the same theme. I have, however, been known to make the odd deviation with regard to prototypes. Various ideas were drawn up, but you know how it is —

The view from inside the winding house, shortly before demolition, looking out over the edge of the incline. The crossing of the track is clearly visible, as are the blades of the point where the two incline tracks converge. In the top right is the guide pulley to lift the cable from the underside of the winding drum clear of the summit of the incline, whilst the cable from the top passed between the vertical guides to the left. The brake lever can just be seen outside on the extreme left. RODNEY STENNING

sometimes the ideas just don't gel, and for some time the project was put on hold. I still wanted to build the winding house, so in the end, I decided not to build a complete layout, just a small scenic diorama small enough to have displayed at home. I've not felt the need to have an operable model railway at home for many years, but I do find it is nice to have something just to look at from time to time — a bit like a nice painting. Small set-pieces or dioramas need not be very large, nor encroach too much into a relatively small living room.

The general appearance of the scene is shown well in the Boyd book and the pho-

tos also give fairly clear views of the winding house, but, just when you think you have all the necessary information for a project, you discover gaping holes in your knowledge. This was no exception. I had nothing about the inside of the house and the rail crossing. Fortunately, a chance meeting at an exhibition brought forth drawings and photos of the winding drum and braking arrangement of similar structures, and my good friend Rodney Stenning came up with a photo of the inside of the Abergynolwyn structure, so I felt confident about at least trying to make a reasonably accurate model.

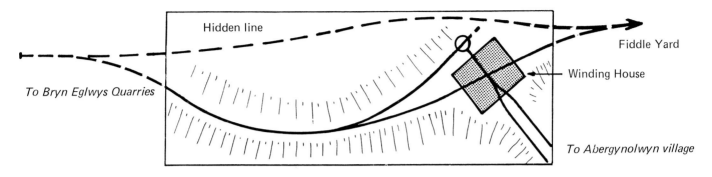

Hidden line

To Bryn Eglwys Quarries

Fiddle Yard

Winding House

To Abergynolwyn village

Not to scale

The eventual scheme consisted of a scene depicting the top of the village incline, the winding house and a short piece of the TR's mineral extension passing through the winding house and along a 'shelf' cut into the hillside. Even a confined location such as this was a bit too large for me to model scale size, so the result was a sort of foreshortened caricature, hopefully capturing the atmosphere and characteristics of the actual setting. There was not enough space to model the full length of the loop around the rear of the house, so this was truncated beyond the turntable, and a covered van, modelled in low relief, positioned to obstruct the view at this point. I reckoned on there being enough trees growing on the hillside to hide the scenic break at the 'top' end, and the line and loop would be partially hidden by the winding house and more trees at the other. The incline tracks were also to disappear behind more foliage in the right foreground.

The whole scene was 4ft long by about 18in deep and housed within an openfronted display box with removable Perspex sliding doors on the front, which, for home use and storage, protected it from dust, but when it was taken out to the occasional exhibition, the doors were removed. Lighting was integral, on a hinged pelmet panel, and consisted of a total of 580 watts of tungsten daylight bulbs — four 100 watt and three 60 watt that gave out a terrific light, but also got very hot! A removable top cover, used at home to keep the dust out, was always removed when the lights were on to let heat escape.

I may seem to be a little paranoid about dust, but some years ago I built a layout

The base unit, showing the thin ply supporting framework. This whole unit was later fitted within a ply display box.

for home use and was very aware of the amount of house dust that collected on it — and that was in a little-used spare room. I decided that this one would be properly protected from the outset, especially as it was to be housed in a room that was in general use.

Although essentially a static diorama, it could be operated if needs be by the attachment of a fiddle yard at one end and a kick-back spur at the other — giving access to a hidden through-line at the rear. The provision of this through-line enabled empty slate wagons, having been pushed through the scene 'up to the quarry', to be hauled back to the fiddle yard via the hidden line. Replacement wagons with slate loads could then be propelled to the kick-back and then hauled down the line and through the scene, 'towards the wharf at Towyn' (back to the fiddle yard).

Unfortunately this was not exactly an absorbing operation, from either the operator's or viewer's point of view. I think it was the four days at York that eventually persuaded me to do away with the fiddle yard altogether and fit a shuttle unit (mine was obtained from Modelex), which enabled a train to quietly crawl to-and-fro through the scene as a background to a scenic demonstration.

From the modelling point of view, the scene did not really break any new ground, although I had never tackled anything so scenic before. I decided, as I always do — but not always with successful results — to try and keep the weight to an absolute minimum. To this end, the scene was built on a 6mm ply table top that formed the trackbed, and this was supported on 4mm ply scenic contours, with lightening holes cut out. A

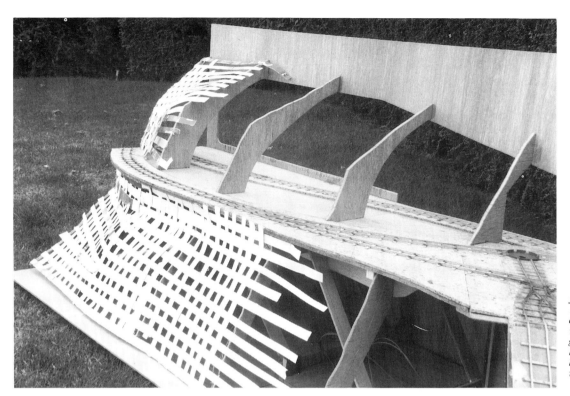

The start of the scenic foundation. Card strips (from cereal packets) are interlaced and tacked down with a hot glue gun and were followed by about three layers of plaster bandage to form the surface.

backing piece, also of 4mm ply, was then added to the full height of the scene, and supported more scenic contours above the track bed. This whole unit was then screwed onto the base of the display case and eventually the rest of the case built around it.

The track was tackled first and this was laid on a cork underlay. The gauge of the Tal-y-llyn Railway was reckoned to be about 2ft 3in which comes close to 16mm in 7mm scale. In the past I had always used 16.5mm gauge to conventional OO standards, but it gives a fair amount of lateral movement with some of the fine-treaded wheelsets supplied in many kits. This caused me a problem as I like to use Alex Jackson couplings and these rely on the stock having minimal side-slop. The wheels could have been moved out on the axles to, say, 15mm back-to-back, but all the stock was existing and I was reluctant to tamper with reliable running equipment. I then thought of the smaller check-rail gap used in EM and the difference of 1.5mm between the 16.5mm back-to-back and the gauge of 18mm (now 18.2mm) so I decided to reduce the gauge to 16mm and keep the back-to-back dimension at 14.5mm. This, of course, had the added advantage of making it closer to the prototype dimension, but would defy anyone to be able to spot a difference of 0.5mm!

The 7mm Narrow Gauge Association publish data sheets outlining the various track gauges, and the relevant standards that are conventionally used by narrow gauge modellers to replicate the vast number of different gauges used on prototype narrow gauge lines. The most popular gauge from the modelling point of view is 16.5mm, which is generally known as 0-16.5, but many products are also available for 14mm gauge and, more recently, there has been a developing interest in 21mm gauge. Unlike specialist groups such as the Scalefour Society or EM Gauge Society, the 7mm Narrow Gauge Association does not represent just one gauge or standard, but caters for all narrow gauges modelled around the scale of 7mm/ft. That said, I don't know anyone else in the Association working to 16mm gauge, although I'm sure I'm not the only oddball!

The Tal-y-llyn track was always flat-bottom rail spiked down, but originally chairs were also dispersed within each 21ft length and the rail ends supported in 'joint chairs'. These were not a success and an ongoing job of drilling the rail ends at each joint and substituting fish-plates was put in hand, although this task was not completed on the mineral line. I decided to try and represent this track with joint chairs and used Peco flat-bottom rail soldered to brass rivets in ply sleepers — the Brook Smith system. C&L chairs were used (cosmetically) in the relevant positions, but because of the flat-bottom rail they had to be carved out at the back of the base before fixing — a very tedious job but well worth the effort.

As the bulk of the scene was to be the hillside, the basic ground shape was made using a lattice of card strips cut from old cereal boxes tacked in place with a hot glue gun. A surface of Modroc (plaster bandage) was then applied and allowed to dry out thoroughly. There were to be a number of rocky outcrops and this was something I hadn't modelled before, so I sought advice from Brian Champion of Set Scenes who suggested trying a latex rubber mould and casting the rocks 'wet' onto the hillside. Brian suggested a suitable plaster — Versitex — and I obtained some liquid latex from EMA Model Supplies and set about making a mould over a piece of stone from the garden. The latex is painted on to build up about ten coats, allowing about an hour between coats, then given a day or two to dry right through. It can then be peeled off and, after dusting the mould with talc, is ready for use. With thoughts of emulating Laurel and Hardy during a slapstick scene, I filled the mould and waited for the moment before quickly placing it onto the surface. There were to be no more dry runs. This time it was for real. The plaster was left until it was judged, as best as I could, to be just starting to set — not too sloppy, but not too solid either — and then . . .

The winding house with a steel-sided wagon waiting to be lowered down to the village.

After clearing up the mess . . . no, it wasn't quite that bad, as some castings turned out very well and even those that weren't so perfect could easily be partially covered in undergrowth at a later stage. Painting the rock faces was with washes of thinned-down acrylic paint from the Tamiya range, finished off after drying with some dry-brushing to highlight and create shadows in appropriate places. The use of Tamiya paints was not crucial but I just happen to get on with them for scenic work. These acrylics dry very fast and I find them ideal for applying washes or for dry-brushing. They are not so suitable, however, where a flat and even finish is called for.

The main subject of the diorama is the winding house. The real structure was built of slate blocks, as are most buildings in the area, and after its demolition in 1968, the reclaimed material was used for improvements at Abergynolwyn station. The model was built in my favoured method of Das-coated ply — Das Pronto being pressed onto the surface of the structure and then, when dry, scribed to represent the slate blocks. Because the

The basic shell of the winding house. The ply structure was covered in Das Pronto (held on with a little PVA glue) and then the slate blocks scribed into the surface. For some reason this was photographed with the units the wrong way round and shows the inside face.

The completed winding house ready for installation. The brake mechanism can be seen loose in this photo, but the base of the handle (on the right) was buried in the hillside when it was fixed in position.

The underside of the winding house, showing the winding drum with cables attached. The cable from the top of the drum ran between large timbers for guidance but the cable from the underside had to be deflected over an underslung pulley to get the correct alignment down the incline.

After the winding house was demolished, the winding drum was left on the site to blend in gradually with the surroundings. This photo was taken in 1991.

tracks pass through the building on all four sides (and cross in the middle), there was no hiding the interior and this also required the scribing treatment. I decided to make the structure walls as two units, each like an arch and joined by the roof, which was also going to make the installation of the 'working' winding drum a little easier. The original intention was to make the top of the incline (all that showed of it) work, with wagons being hauled up and lowered down in a very gentle manner. Unfortunately, it was the 'gentle' criteria that I could not meet to my liking: because the incline was far too steep, the power required to haul the wagons to the top was enough to launch them as they cleared the summit, when the resistance suddenly diminished, whilst the one being lowered plummeted at an equal rate of knots. After a couple of frustrating weekends playing about with the mechanics of this, I threw in the towel and decided to leave this sort of thing to Dave Rowe!

There were to be quite a few trees within the scene and these were made with multi-strand electrical wire. A number of lengths of about 2ft were cut off and after being stripped were twisted together at the base to form the trunks. These were also bound with fuse-wire to prevent them from untwisting, then soldered up solid. The branches were twisted together, but these tended not to need the fuse-wire binding, and gradually the work moved out towards the twigs at the ends. The bare trees had to be fairly well detailed because I did not want to show a full complement of foliage, preferring to model an autumn scene with many of the leaves already fallen. If the trees had been too full of foliage, the small scene could easily have turned into a dense forest and it would have looked far too cramped. Being able to see through them to the back of the scene has helped to give an impression of space.

With the locos and rolling stock already existing and relatively modest requirements for trackwork and wiring, the bulk of the modelling was making the scenery. With only 4ft of length to consider, it was very pleasurable to be able to spend time building up the depth, from a basic ground layer followed by moss, rotting leaves and undergrowth to longer straggly grass and bracken. In all, the display took about twelve months to put together and probably as much as half of that time was spent on the scenic work.

TR No. 2 Dolgoch, *hauling a pair of empty slate wagons towards the quarries.*

No. 1 resting in the shadows.

Tal-y-llyn *bringing a loaded train down from the quarry.*

Dolgoch hauling a loaded slate train along the ledge towards the winding house.

Dolgoch *propelling a pair of empty slate wagons towards the quarries.*

Dolgoch *standing outside the winding house.*

At the York exhibition, a visitor remarked that there was no wildlife within the scene, which was very true. The next display to ours, and within earshot, was the John & Gerry Show, and the comment had been duly noted by Gerry Hall, who offered to make us a woodpecker. A while later, a small parcel arrived containing the beautifully-carved and delicately painted bird complete with mounting instructions — a truly wonderful piece of work. But, as recalled in MRJ No.59, what we had not realised at the time was that Gerry had first made it to 4mm scale!

The intention of keeping the whole scene reasonably small was so that it could be displayed at home, mounted on a wall and supported on a couple of microwave oven brackets. This was the case for about three years, but eventually I decided even this was a bit too overpowering for the small room it was in, and made up my mind to try and find it another home. This was achieved with the help of Derek Allen of the Talyllyn Railway Preservation Society, and I am very proud that the scene is now on display in their museum at Towyn Wharf station.

In reality there was a loop line behind the winding house from which a wagon turntable made a connection with the incline. On the model this loop was truncated beyond the turntable and a covered van used as a 'view block'.

The top of the incline with a steel-sided mineral wagon ready to be lowered to the village.

Scratchbuilt LSWR Dropside in 7mm

*Taking inspiration from the prototype's performance characteristics, DAVE GOSLING
devised, among other things, an invisible, independent springing system for his
exquisitely detailed South Western three-planker:*

The LSWR built around 200 three-plank drop-side wagons of 7 or 10 tons capacity between 1887 and 1912, with either timber or Fox pressed steel underframes. At least 183 passed into SR ownership under Diagram 1301. Most of the steel variety, constructed 1896–9, were subsequently employed as ballast wagons in the Engineer's Department and had an overall height 1¼in lower than their timber counter-parts, and underframes 3in shallower at 9in. The 1880s saw a number of the wooden-framed variety shipped to the Bodmin and Wadebridge before that company was physi-cally connected to its parent.

This prototype proved the ideal choice for this, my first serious essay in 7mm scale modelling. A recent convert from P4, the adoption of ScaleSeven standards was inescapable. In addition, I wanted to begin my work in the new scale by establishing a stan-dard construction methodology with which I was satisfied before progressing with further models. Every attention is commonly given to wagon/coach/loco bodies but it is too often assumed that, as long as they are then placed on a few wheels, no more need be done. Wagon bodies only constrain the goods – underframes have to do all the real work. Every component is designed for a practical reason and I've always felt that we modellers should treat them with a bit of respect, endeavouring to represent the prototype characteristics in miniature form. That being my opinion, I concentrated my attention on the underframe.

Drawgear and buffers are soft-sprung; on trains of any length such a wagon placed near the locomotive will, on propelling, compress its buffers and, on hauling, visibly move the coupling away from the buffer beam if the train is snatched – though not to the extent that it is hanging out like a thirsty tongue! Proprietary components, I have found, are gen-erally too stiffly sprung. The wheelsets on the model are also softly sprung. Consequently, all the wheels are on the track at all times and the wagon does not lurch over points and rail joints, a propensity not removed, incidentally, from vehicles equipped with compensation-only underframes.

It was important, however, not to meet these requirements only at the expense of visual accuracy. A case in point is the currently oft-used ruse of separating wagon/coach springs from their associated axleboxes, leaving a noticeable gap, as a prerequisite for the instal-lation of some compensated systems. I feel that it is important to safeguard, as far as possible, both illusion and accuracy. The most immaculately painted livery adorning the most exquisitely detailed body can be ruined for me by having a great big gap where no gap should be.

CONSTRUCTION

My design parameters demanded that all items be easily and quickly constructed from readily available materials and that all 'tricks' – that is departures from prototype practice – should be, as far as possible, invisible. Firstly, I equipped the wagon with a brass sub-chassis. This feature enables the model to be painted more easily since most prototypes have a defi-nite livery break around solebar level. It also provides for greater strength where it is most necessary. To this sub-chassis are attached the W-irons/leaf spring castings with integral or separate axleboxes and very nearly all of the brake gear. Provision is made for the draw and buffing gear to be anchored through this frame as well as passing through the plastic head-stock. The general layout of parts (*Photo 1*) is fairly self-explanatory. The frame is soldered from 6.3mm × 1mm brass drilled at the ends to allow buffer spindles and drawbar to pass through. The buffers are from the ABS range, the spindles being replaced by 1.7mm O/D brass tube threaded 10BA where it passes behind the buffer beam in order to accept the retaining nut. The buffers have to be remov-able in order to be able to separate the sub-chassis from the body since the spindles pass through both. The operating spring – 0.035mm steel guitar wire – is cranked at either end to pass into the tube. In order to operate, the wire must also pass through the extended shank of the drawbar. Nothing revolutionary here, just the smallest of modifications of existing ideas in order to suit present circumstances.

In tackling the wheelset assemblies, I dis-counted the possibility of my being able to make reliable working leaf springs so arranged for the springing to be situated behind the W-irons but to be constructed in such a way as to be invisible from normal viewing angles. An axle-bearing sub-assembly was constructed

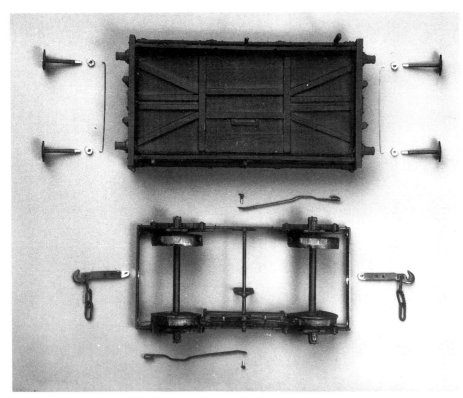

The main component parts of the wagon. On assembly, the sub-chassis is retained in position by the buffer spindles and coupling passing through both the cosmetic and functional buffer beams, the brake lever subsequently being attached.

The cosmetic W-iron and its functional U-iron sister. The spring locates in the slots cut in the underside of the brass solebar; the wheels, if accurately fitted, ensure a smooth up and down action with no floppy sideplay. The rear of the axlebox has been drilled or milled out to permit about 2mm of movement.

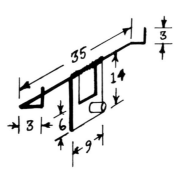

Fig. 1. SPRINGING UNIT

Dimensions in millimetres.
Dimensions of U-iron to be modified to suit vehicle.

from shim brass cut to imitate the shape of the central pillars of the W-iron (see *Photo 2*) producing a sort of U-iron. A hole was drilled in the lower part of this to accept a Slater's bearing within which would run Slater's open-spoked wheels, turned to ScaleSeven standards, and normally available, I believe, to order. The axlebox/W-iron castings I was using (ABS) came with separately-cast axle-boxes. The LSWR flat-sided shape made it easy for me to place them in the pillar drill machine vice and deftly elongate the bearing holes to accommodate the movement of the brass bearing. Thus, the whole of the axlebox, as seen from the outside, fulfils no functional purpose. Guitar wire was again used for springing. The third (or G) string on a steel-strung acoustic guitar is wound, usually, with bronze. Cut a length of wire about a couple of inches long. Place one end in a vice, grasp the winding with a pair of pliers and pull. The core will twirl as the winding spins off. Remove less than half the winding, turn the wire around in the vice and remove an amount from the other end, leaving about 9mm of winding in the middle. The wire is then soldered to the top of the U-iron. The inclusion of the winding, being flooded with solder, produces a very solid joint; without the winding everything would very soon come adrift.

The wire is then bent as shown in *Fig 1*. Cuts 1mm deep are made in the underside of the brass underframe 17.5mm either side of the central mounting point of the axlebox assembly to accommodate a spring 35mm long. Corresponding grooves are cut in the inside of the cosmetic plastic solebars to allow for sufficient spring flexing. The finished assembly can be tweaked in order to provide for even spring pressures acting upon all wheels and, by careful easing of the axlebox castings, wheel removal is possible though not recommended too often.

Mike King, one of the authors of *An Illustrated History of SR Wagons*, informs me that there is no evidence of any LSWR drop-side wagon being equipped with Panter's cross-lever brake since, presumably, those sides would foul the linkage. The single-sided Morton gear consequently modelled began life as ABS castings but, neat as these are, they are of overscale thickness and suffer from one particularly unfortunate drawback – the twin pushrods of the prototype are represented by a single rod, albeit the thickness of the casting being roughly the correct thickness for the two rods together but having, of course, no gap. I was consequently obliged to make them from scratch.

Cutting the parts from sheet metal was too daunting; strip metal could conceivably have been used but is hell to drill. The alternative was 20-thou styrene. Brake blocks, push rods, brake hangers and vee-hangers are contenders for this medium in 7mm scale but they are subject to breakage by clumsy fingers during the building of other parts of the vehicle, so they should be incorporated as late in the constructional sequence as is practicable. After completion they appear satisfactorily robust except in the case of the model being carelessly dropped from a great height or suffering from a spectacularly devastating collision.

Components requiring bending – brake levers and guides, safety loops, door stops – have to be fashioned, tediously, from metal, the tapering of the brake lever being especially taxing. The appearance of the final product is, however, worth the endeavour to emulate the prototype as far as is practicable. With this in mind, the middle vee-hanger is also modelled, locating in, but not attached to, a channel in the floor of the vehicle made from strips of styrene (*Photo 3*).

The transverse operating rod is brass tube tapped at either end to facilitate attaching by 14BA bolts to the cam mechanism, on the braked side, and the brake lever on the other. Before fixing the bolt, a piece of fuse wire is

The underside of the assembled wagon. The positioning of the springs is clearly seen with the cuts in the inner, brass frame and the slots in the outer, styrene solebar being visible. Note the middle V-hanger nestling in its locating channel.

Left: *The springing units, operating between the wheels and the W-iron, are not apparent even in this close-up end-on view. I think that using real chains and persevering with finicky items like individual hooks, rather than adopting a representational approach, results in a more rewarding and satisfactory end product.* Right: *The Morton gear in close-up, showing the twin push rods and cam operating mechanism. Breakage during construction has resulted in a less than perfect finish – next time I'll leave them until last. Final painting improved matters, the end result justifying the amount of time spent on detail work.*

A general view of the model before painting.

wrapped around some guitar wire and fashioned into a split pin. When soldered into the slot in the head of the bolt and cleaned up, the split pin conveniently gives the impression of having been passed through the bolt. It should be explained that, since the brake lever guides are fixed to the outer styrene solebar, and the vee-hangers are secured to the inner brass sub-chassis, the brake levers should be threaded through the guides after offering up the sub-chassis to the body assembly and before screwing up the split-pinned bolt. More guitar wire is bent to shape and soldered to the tube around the push rods to simulate a wire safety loop; the push rods themselves, being styrene, can easily be drilled to simulate the many holes used for correct brake block adjustment.

Body construction is straightforward, made mainly from 30 or 40-thou sheet, suitably scribed. Bolt detail found on strapping is embossed before the strap is cut from 10-thou sheet; larger bolt detail is represented by drilling in the appropriate places and gluing in lacemaker's pins, snipping them off and tidying with a file. The chains securing the doors are made from the finest silver chain I could readily obtained from the local jewellers; cost only £2 or £3 for a worthwhile length. A length of the ubiquitous guitar wire is wound round a suitable diameter screw or piece of wire, then snipped off to make a loop. This was fixed, on the one hand to the chain, on the other to a piece of wire flattened at the end and carefully drilled. This was then glued into a hole drilled in the angle strap at the ends of the sides. The hooks attached to the ends are also made from brass wire, flattened at the tip and drilled to take a filed-down pin. They slot into a loop built into the construction of the wagon side itself. The tarpaulin cleats are made by cutting out small triangle shapes from 10-thou styrene. On these are glued small circles punched from similar material by a leather punch. These come out a little dished, as per prototype. This propensity enables fine fuse wire to be carefully wound around the cleat, allowing a tarpaulin to be fitted where necessary.

CONCLUSION
As construction progressed, mental notes were made as to changes in procedure which I might consider when tackling future projects. The most obvious was to make the sub-chassis sides from thicker brass, enabling them to double as solebars, whilst leaving the headstocks modelled in styrene. The springs could then simply be located into holes drilled in the underside of the solebars, with small sawcuts joining the holes to the inner edge of the solebar in order to allow the spring to locate, out of sight, behind. Since the brake lever guides and door stops are metal, they would benefit from being soldered to a metal solebar rather than pinned to one of styrene.

Although the cast W-irons have been chamfered to improve their end-on viewing characteristics, a better solution would be to utilise brass etchings. However, I cannot locate a source of cast LSWR axleboxes and leaf springs not already attached to W-irons, though I suppose these could be carefully cut away from composite castings. Manufacturers of whole wagon or brake-gear only kits please note: the ideal constructional materials are, I suggest, etched W-irons, vee-hangers and most of the brake rigging; cast axleboxes, springs and brake blocks. An additional visual benefit accrues from the separation of the springs from the W-irons.

'SUNBURY'

FRANCIS SAMISH builds a tiny 4mm narrow gauge tank based on a Roxey kit:

In 1915, Kerr-Stuart built three little 2ft gauge 0–4–2 tanks for the Metropolitan Water Board to transport coal from a Thameside wharf at Hampton (opposite Platt's Eyot) to the boiler-houses of its two pumping stations. The 4mm scale model of *Sunbury* – Kerr-Stuart 2368 in miniature – is based around the Roxey Mouldings kit, though uses a Bachmann 0–4–0 N-gauge saddle tank mechanism instead of the recommended Ibertren unit. False outside frames were made up from about 20-thou brass, secured by solder to a single copper-clad stretcher fixed by a single screw under the smokebox, and fitted with a bridgepiece at the rear, doubling as a keeper plate for the trailing wheels. No pony truck as such is used.

In order to keep the width of the cylinders as close to scale as practicable, no front flycranks or coupling rods are fitted either. In operation, this subterfuge is virtually invisible. Valve gear and rods were made by first measuring the centre-to-centre dimensions, marking-out on ½in brass sheet, drilling out, and then carefully sawing and filing to shape. Only at the final stage is the embryo coupling rod or whatever sawn off the supporting sheet. When judged satisfactory, each part is then 'wiped' with solder to simulate burnished steel.

Superstructure construction is nothing much out of the ordinary. Low-melt solder is employed for securing the major components, with the detailing items added from tinned brass wire and suchlike. Fusewire served for the

handrails and pipework since it can so easily be tweaked with watchmakers' tweezers to follow boiler contours. Lamp irons were again sawn and filed from ½in sheet, with brass turnings for the lubricators, whistle and safety-valve casings.

Copper paint sufficed for the blower pipe and chimney cap, though the smokebox door locking handle is solder wiped once more – a poor attempt at a crossed-spoke wheel. Yet as this particular component is a mere 2mm across, I confess to having had no sleepless nights on this score!

The lining out (ahhh . . . the lining out) took nearly a week to achieve, and was carried out with waterslide lining over a gloss-varnished basecoat of GWR green. To conform to cab roof and boiler top curvature, the strip is cut into tiny 1mm segments, each applied individually, and then the gaps touched in by brush with the final yellow/black/yellow colour scheme. No easy way out existed with the cab and tank sides – not to mention the sandboxes – and here the corners had to be lined out by hand. At times like these one becomes vexed at the complexity of late Edwardian locomotive adornment, but there is no denying that *Sunbury* looks the part from normal viewing distance!

Roxey Mouldings of 58 Dudley Road, Walton-on-Thames, Surrey KT12 2JU still market the kit (ref LOK 3). For further information on the railway itself, Paul Webb and Brian Clarke's monograph: *The Metropolitan Water Board Narrow Gauge Railway* (1986) is recommended.

HAMPSTEAD NORRIS

FOUR OUTINGS AND A FUNERAL

Not many of you will have seen this layout which was based on Hampstead Norris station on the GWR's former Didcot, Newbury & Southampton Railway in the 1920s. It only went to four exhibitions before being consigned to the council tip.

It was bought in about 1978 in an unfinished state by the embryonic Bucks & Oxon Group (BOG for short, but now known as the North Bucks Group of the Scalefour Society). As purchased, only the bare baseboards and trackwork existed, together with an almost complete station building. The rather distinctive baseboards consisted of a single 'scenic' board, all of 9ft long, with a 3ft fiddle yard permanently hinged at each end, all in best municipal 2in x 1in and chipboard. The entire ensemble was duly loaded on the roof rack of a Cortina for the precarious 40 mile journey home, the overhanging boards flexing gently in tune with the suspension. This process un-nerved the passengers to such an extent that a decision was swiftly taken to cut the layout in half to make it more manageable. So, after a suitable dose of brave pills, a large saw was introduced to the centre of the 9ft board. Since this also marked the centre of the loco release crossover, the running qualities of the layout were not noticeably enhanced . . .

In acquiring a half-built layout, the then three-strong group were taking on someone else's model of a station with

Purchased unfinished, sawn in half, sold, bought back and prettified, the P4 layout Hampstead Norris had a blighted life. It managed four exhibition showings before heading into the skip. It wasn't perfect but, says MIKE CLARK, it did look nice . . .

The layout as first purchased but after being sawn in half!

The Dean Goods, based on the Mallard kit, was built especially for the layout by Gerry Beale.

which they were only vaguely familiar. Broadening their knowledge was made much easier by the coincidentally simultaneous preparation of one of the earliest Wild Swan books, *The Didcot, Newbury & Southampton Railway*. Hampstead Norris was not the most prolifically photographed station in the country, so the photographs that this brought to light proved invaluable in creating the right appearance in the station area.

The layout was lengthened and finished scenically and electrically by the group and taken to three local exhibitions. It was then sold, only to be re-purchased by group member Andy Wiles some years later. It was then scenically revised and went to Scaleforum North at Huddersfield before being consigned to the skip when Andy moved to the States.

When Andy acquired the layout, it was decided to upgrade the scenic work. This involved replacing the lint grass with

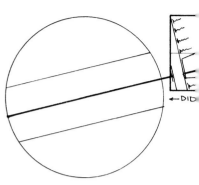

A view of the cutting from the public side. The modelling of the chalk sides was done by Gerry Beale (now lost to 7mm modelling). The 'Barnum' and train of clerestory coaches were built by Andy Wiles.

A view of the station (with the end board missing) with the '850' shunting the yard. This shot demonstrates how large-radius curves create the illusion of space on a model. The foreground trees made the viewer peer round them, giving a variety of 'framed' views. They created a curiosity and made spectators search the layout, and more was probably seen as a result.

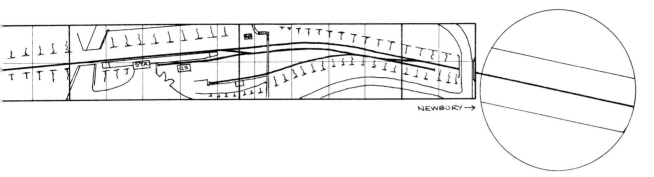

NEWBURY →

A closer view of the excellent long footbridge which was built by Adrian Gray and now resides in my loft awaiting a new home.

The '850' with the pick-up goods in the loop and ready to depart. This shot shows how trees (both foreground and background) framed the view and concentrated the eye on the train — an important consideration as far as the Geordie contingent in the group are concerned. It's the only way to get them to look at funny little green and brass engines.

carpet underlay and modelling the full-size trees as they existed around 1920. An aerial photograph of the station made this easy to get right and only one or two trees were added to either help frame views or for artistic effect.

All the photographs reproduced here show the layout with its revised scenery. One batch was taken in Andy's house in Crich where it was not possible to erect the whole layout, whilst the second batch was taken at the exhibition in Huddersfield before punters were let in one morning.

The trackwork which the group had inherited when they originally purchased the layout was not entirely satisfactory and the ripsaw through the middle didn't

Looking up from the road with the 'Barnum' entering the station. The undergrowth in the foreground was made from stretched-out horsehair, sprayed with glue and covered with fine scatter material. The grass on the embankment was made of carpet felt and all stuck down one weekend during a blizzard in Crich when four of the group managed to get themselves snowed up for two days. (We left when the pub ran out of beer.)

This view from the end of the platform shows some of the less than ideal trackwork inherited by the group. The train is Andy's 'Barnum' and coaches (gold medal winner at the MEE in the 1980s).

Andy Wiles' 'Barnum' and train trundling into the station under the long footbridge.

help! It should have been rebuilt, but it was not until the layout was re-acquired by Andy that it was 'sort of sorted' as the saying goes.

Well, that is a brief history of the layout. Before being deposited in the council Biffa, Andy retrieved the footbridge, buildings, trees and the exquisite road sign which had been modelled and lettered by Bob How. (When asked recently if he could do the lettering again, he replied that he was not even sure he could see the sign now, never mind the lettering.)

That's about it. All the rest is in the photographs. It looked very nice, ran OK, but was dead boring to operate.

Andy Wiles' beautiful '850' class saddle tank (see MRJ Compendium No. 2) with a train of Bob How's superb private owner coal wagons running through the landscape.

The benefits of a backscene when viewing the layout from track level are apparent in this photo of the coal train ambling out from under the bridge (transplanted from its real location about half a mile away).

MODEL RAILWAY DRAWING BY COMPUTER

WIM HARTHOORN looks at the options, and demonstrates the possibilities:

The computer is the defining technology of the late twentieth century, much as the steam engine was that of the nineteenth. Many modellers these days have their own PCs or work in offices or schools[1] which have them, and may be unaware that some of the applications available on the standard IBM PC compatible can produce very acceptable drawings of railway subjects with little effort. The purpose of this article is to look at some of the common drawing software that may well be available to a railway modeller, and to assist its usefulness.

TYPES OF DRAWING SOFTWARE

Drawing software comes in two forms, bitmap packages and vector drawing packages. **Bitmap** drawings are made up of a grid of tiny dots called pixels, rather like old-fashioned newspaper photographs. It might be assumed that drawings made up like this would appear crude, but since even the humblest desk-jet printer can now print black and white drawings to a resolution of 300 dots to the inch, the results are as sharp as the finest Rotring pen. The advantage of bitmap packages is that they are intuitive to use. The disadvantages are many — they are tedious for complicated drawings, lack sophistication and even the simplest drawing fills up an inordinate amount of computer disk space.

Bitmap drawing software is, however, essential for modifying images scanned into the computer using a hand-held or flat-bed scanner, but more on this subject later.

Vector drawing packages are more complex. The computer records each line or area of the drawing as a mathematical formula covering length, direction, curvature and other attributes. From the computer's point of view, this is much more efficient in the use of disk space. From the modeller's point of view, this type of drawing package is more flexible in use once the initial familiarisation is complete.

'Why use a computer?' is a question that could be, should be and isn't asked throughout whole swathes of modern life. Frequently, pencil and paper can be superior. However, computers excel in three areas — storage and retrieval of information, consistency of results, and time-saving in repetitive tasks. When using a computer to produce drawings for railway modellers, these benefits are all present. Take the example of a coach drawing. There may be upward of a dozen identical windows, or eight to ten identical compartments. Using a computer, a repeating object is drawn once and then copied speedily for the rest. Another example is that of a coach set. An all third and a composite may well have identical overall dimensions, identical underframes and only differ in the layout of the compartments. Using a computer here, the common features can be produced first and then saved and used as the basis for producing the different members of the set. Finally, it has to be said that computers do not misread dimensions, smear ink under the ruler, or spill coffee on the paper. Should the human operator make mistakes, these can be rectified, at worst by returning to the previously saved copy.

DRAWING WITH A BITMAP PACKAGE

Apart from modifying scanned images, I would not bother with bitmap packages were it not for the fact that nearly every PC shipped in the last three years has a free copy of one such package already installed. This is the humble Paintbrush utility that is part of Microsoft Windows. Paintbrush has a number of potentially useful features: for example, a line tool which can draw lines accurately between two points or exactly vertical or horizontal, a box tool, and a tool to draw circles and ellipses. However, it does not have any scaling, and, because it is a bitmap package, making changes is not easy. However, with patience, Paintbrush can be used to produce working drawings of a wagon or coach body to a scale as small as 3mm/ft, particularly if the source information is sketchy.

In order to show how Paintbrush can be used, a drawing of a Victorian third class carriage has been produced as an example and four stages in the drawing process shown.

The first step is to draw rulers along the bottom and up the left-hand side. Paintbrush has no indicated dimensions, and scaling a picture has to be done at the printing stage. However, it is important that the relative dimensions are correct. Paintbrush allows zooming in to show the individual pixels, so in this example I made each pixel equivalent to 0.1mm, and by marking off each tenth pixel, obtained a 1mm spacing on the rulers.

Once the rulers were drawn, a set of boxes and circles were drawn to give the basic outline of the carriage. Where the wheels are behind the solebar, the eraser tool was used to rub out the unwanted parts of the circle. Approximate time to this stage was twenty minutes, most of which was spent on drawing the rulers. For the next drawing, the same rulers could be used, saving some fifteen minutes.

This particular carriage has four identical compartments. Windows are fortunately square, which means that the box drawing tool can be used. Rounded corners would be a little more difficult, but only because the radius would need careful adjustment. The circle drawing tool would be used and three-quarters of the circle subsequently rubbed out. Time to draw one compartment — approximately fifteen minutes.

Because all compartments are identical, the time taken to copy the compartment drawn, and then to position the three copies on the drawing, is under five minutes.

Beading and other details can be added. The appearance of the drawing can be improved by applying a light shading to the windows and a darker shading to underframe details.

Further detail work can be done given time and patience, although, with the level of knowledge surviving about this particular vehicle and the lack of clear photographs, this might be of limited relevance. This demonstration drawing took under an hour to this stage.

At this point, the drawing is not to scale. To achieve this, a print has to be taken and then the percentage reduction or enlargement required calculated. A second print is then taken with the appropriate adjustment.

As seen in the demonstration, copy and paste techniques can be used in Paintbrush to speed up the drawing of

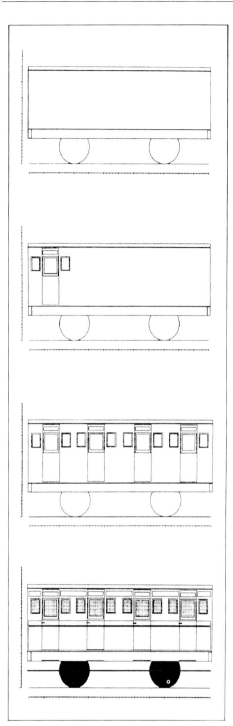

repeated objects such as carriage compartments, ventilators, grab handles, etc. Unfortunately, once placed, they cannot be moved if they overlap other features. This is not a problem, however, with the vector drawing packages as the objects have separate identities.

SIMPLE VECTOR DRAWING PACKAGE

As with Paintbrush, many office PCs have an adequate vector drawing package installed on them. Since 1993 Microsoft have included a utility known as

Microsoft Draw with their word processing and spreadsheet software. Microsoft Draw is not an independent product; it can only be used as part of a word-processing document, or spreadsheet, but as many modellers may actually have access to it without being aware of the fact, it is worth having a look at it.[2]

Draw has the same line and box drawing tools as Paintbrush, but it has major advantages in that scaling is possible and different items in the drawing can be treated as independent objects and moved around and sized without affecting their neighbours.

Scaling is achieved because Draw has movable guidelines, which are analogous to the sliding ruler and set-square on a good quality drawing board. These guidelines give dimensions in centimetres theoretically to three decimal places, in practice to a quarter of a millimetre, although this can be nominal as differences can creep in during printing. One very useful feature of the guides is that objects will 'snap' to them, making accurate positioning quick and easy.

One good use of computer drawing packages, because of their ability to make changes so easily, is the production of drawings of obscure vehicles where the information to hand is no more than a few dimensions, a poor quality photograph or two and a bit of basic knowledge of the particular railway company's practice. As an example, consider the SER's curiously named 'Vacuum' thirds of 1893. The information to hand is quite limited. The underframes are known to be 33ft 10½in long, and it is suspected that some were later used for gas tank wagons. If so, there is a Skinley print that may be of some use. It is known that the bodies of the Vacuum thirds were cobbled together from some old four-

wheelers from the 1850s and 1860s, and the photograph in David Gould's book shows a distinct similarity to a service vehicle drawing in one of R. W. Kidner's books on Southern Railway rolling stock. However, it is clear that R. W. Kidner made some assumptions as to the roof height of the vehicle he drew, as it is too high for an 1860s carriage. To produce an acceptable drawing from this amount of information will require quite a bit of trial and error, something for which the computer is better suited than more traditional methods.

The first step is to rough out the drawing using known dimensions and reasonable assumptions based on the dimensions of similar stock.

So far, the use of a computer drawing package has not shown any advantage over a sharp pencil and a ruler, although estimated dimensions like height can be put in, viewed for effect, and stretched or shrunk to see if alternatives look better. The computer now comes into its own as we are now faced with drawing seven compartments, all the same, and after they have been drawn there may be the need to make some small adjustment to all of them. Pencil drawers have rubbers on standby . . .

NOTES
1 The only experience I have of the Acorn PCs that Tescos has provided through its Computers for Schools promotions is of a frustrating summer holiday trying to get one of the blasted things to work. This article only deals with IBM PC-compatible programs.

2 In Microsoft Word for Windows, access Draw as follows (basic familiarity with Windows assumed): Insert — Object — Microsoft Draw (or using keyboard ALT + I, O, select Microsoft Draw with cursor control keys, <enter>)

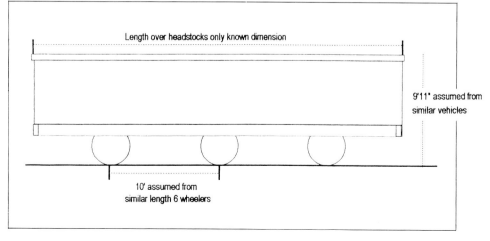

Length over headstocks only known dimension

9'11" assumed from similar vehicles

10' assumed from similar length 6 wheelers

Now in the ideal world, all that would remain to be done is to hit the print key and a superbly accurate print would appear. Unfortunately, what we have here is a piece of software that was designed to draw organisation charts and maybe the odd schematic or office desk layout. Somewhere between producing the diagram and actually printing it, an error of around 5% creeps in. The cure is, as with Paintbrush, to take a test print and then to apply the appropriate adjustment in picture scaling.

'PROPER' DRAWING PACKAGES

So far I have only described a couple of drawing packages that are included free with standard office software. Because these products were bought in by Micro-soft to enhance an otherwise boring application, they lack sophistication and are clumsy in certain respects, especially in being able to produce an accurately scaled print without a fuss. Therefore here are some pointers on specialist drawing packages in case there is a demand out there for more information.

Lotus Freelance: The original version (Freelance 3.1 or Freelance 4 for DOS) was a good drawing package. Unfortunately, the Windows version has been re-packaged for the corporate presentation market, and whilst it may be brilliant for producing slides for the marketing department, it is not as good for real drawing.

Microsoft Powerpoint: Like Freelance for Windows, this is really a presentation graphics package.

Autocad: The original choice for drawing software. However, it's quite pricey and I'm told it's a pig to use.

Corel Draw: Although I have not had any experience of this personally, it is generally reported to be an excellent product but priced at around £350-£400.

Micrografx Windows Draw: Priced at £70 about nine months ago, I haven't seen it lately. It would be a pity if it is no longer available as it is a good budget price bit of drawing software.

There may be other packages available, and the Shareware[3] market has many that may be worth a try for the couple of quid that a shareware trial costs. However, shareware should only be loaded onto a home PC. Where I work it is a disciplinary matter to load unauthorised software onto the company's PCs and I'm told we are relatively relaxed in this respect. I would also point out that terms like budget are relative, I realise that £70 is

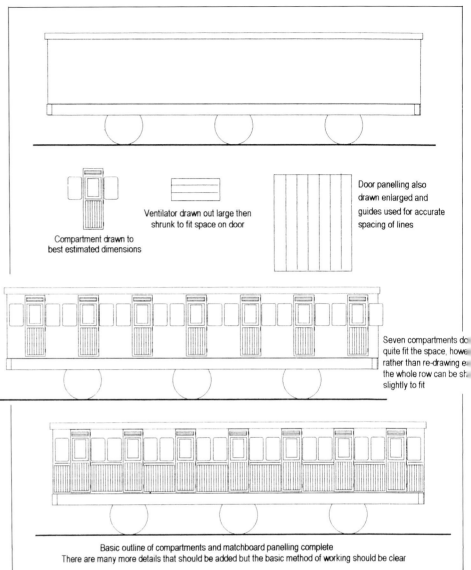

Compartment drawn to best estimated dimensions

Ventilator drawn out large then shrunk to fit space on door

Door panelling also drawn enlarged and guides used for accurate spacing of lines

Seven compartments do quite fit the space, howe rather than re-drawing e the whole row can be sh slightly to fit

Basic outline of compartments and matchboard panelling complete
There are many more details that should be added but the basic method of working should be clear

not budget compared to the thirty-bob Jinty.

For someone who is likely to produce many drawings, the advantages of programs such as the Micrografx one is the greater accuracy of the printed output, a greater range of drawing tools, including a bezier curve tool, more scope for manipulating objects and the ability to import pictures in other formats. The bezier curve tool in particular is essential for accurate drawing of complex curves, for example roof shapes, cab shapes or locomotive splashers. The ability to import drawings in other formats comes into its own if a scanner is available.

SCANNERS AND SCANNED IMAGES

A scanner is basically the input end of a photocopier, but instead of producing a printed output, the output is a bit-map file. This bit-map file can be loaded into

3   For those not familiar with PC terminology, shareware refers to software produced outside of the mainstream companies, frequently by hobbyists. It is generally sold through ads in the PC magazines and the procedure is that the buyer initially pays a nominal sum, £4-£6, which covers the cost of the floppy disks and administration. This then entitles the buyer to a trial period, usually thirty days, at the end of which the software is either deleted off the system or the full fee is paid, typically £50 or there-abouts. The advantage to the buyer is that a software product can be trialled without risking large amounts of money, the advantage to the software vendor is that market-ing overheads are minimised. The disadvantage to the buyer is that shareware is generally bug-ridden. Not surprisingly, given that it takes Microsoft, with all its program-ming resources, a couple of years and several attempts to produce a reasonably bug-free bit of code. What chance does the one-man-and-a-dog shareware outfit have? The disadvantage to the producer is that the system does rely on the honesty of the buyer.

something like Paintbrush and tidied up or modified. Scanners come in different varieties. The cheapest sort is the hand-held sort that is rolled across the picture to be scanned and is limited to an approximately 4in wide strip. These scanners are now around £100, depending on the quality, and are generally shipped with some image manipulating software which can adjust brightness and contrast and even stitch a number of 4in wide strips together. This last process is a bit hit and miss as the join is always obvious.

More expensive scanners are desk mounted and can generally accept A4 sized drawings. The best scanners can also scan in colour. However, with a price tag of approaching £1,000, they are not common in the average office.

SCANNER/DRAWING PACKAGE FOR LOCO DESIGN
Designing a loco mechanism for a scratch-built model requires both accurate positioning of key components relative to each other and an amount of trial and error for the overall layout. However, it would be a major pain to have to redraw a complete motor and transmission set-up every time the angle of mounting was changed to ensure that it will fit under the loco body. A computer is well suited to this kind of juggling and the example here is that of trying to fit a Tenshodo motor into a Manning Wardle saddle tank while keeping the cab area clear. A drawing of the Manning Wardle prototype was found in a magazine and the image scanned in, and Micrografx Windows Draw was used to draw the motor mechanism and for the final design.

OBTAINING THE OUTLINE
An excellent 7mm scale drawing of a Manning Wardle 'I' class (the Selsey tramway MWs) appeared in one of the early issues of *Model Railway Journal*. Using a hand-held scanner, a copy was made and stored as a bit-map image. Then using Paintbrush, most of the detail was wiped out, leaving just an outline.

DESIGNING THE MECHANISM
Not surprisingly, the motor chosen to power this locomotive is the smallest Tenshodo available. Because the small wheels do not allow anything larger than an 18:1 worm drive, a two-stage drive is required. A 2:1 reduction stage using Sharman spur gears is proposed. The drawings here were done in Micrografx Windows Draw and initially measured at four times actual size.

'FITTING' THE MECHANISM
The next step is to overlay the mechanism on the outline of the superstructure and tilting it to get it to fit. This demonstration has only considered the side-on view; obviously the end-on view will have to be considered as well.

SUMMARY
What I have tried to show in this article is that decent quality drawings can now be produced on a standard office computer. For those who have the necessary skill, the traditional drawing board may well continue to be the tool of choice, but even for those people, the ability to produce drawings quickly and accurately and to introduce a bit of trial and error must have some benefits. As I hope I have shown, much of the software may well be around in our place of work or on the PC bought for ourselves or the kids to become 'IT aware'. This article has not set out to be an in-depth evaluation of computer-aided design, but merely to offer a flavour of what may be possible.

This article first appeared in Mixed Traffic, *journal of The 3mm Society.*

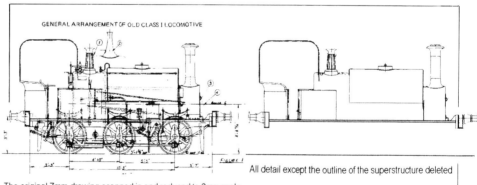

GENERAL ARRANGEMENT OF OLD CLASS I LOCOMOTIVE

All detail except the outline of the superstructure deleted

The original 7mm drawing scanned in and reduced to 3mm scale

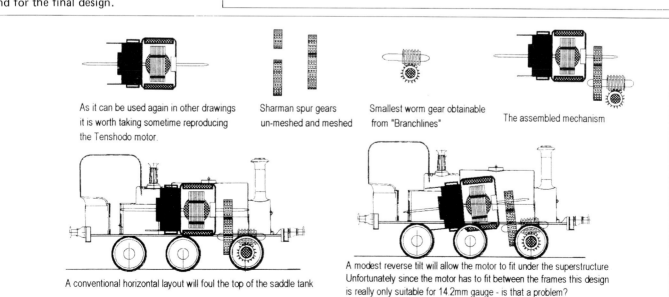

As it can be used again in other drawings it is worth taking sometime reproducing the Tenshodo motor.

Sharman spur gears un-meshed and meshed

Smallest worm gear obtainable from "Branchlines"

The assembled mechanism

A conventional horizontal layout will foul the top of the saddle tank

A modest reverse tilt will allow the motor to fit under the superstructure Unfortunately since the motor has to fit between the frames this design is really only suitable for 14.2mm gauge - is that a problem?

Over thirty models of Great Western locomotives from Captain Kelly's South Devon Railway on display at the Model Railway Club exhibition at Central Hall in 1932.

I approached down the familiar over-grown path, passing a lion-head water spout and lily pool and into a wooded glade dappled in sunlight, my small son at my side. Two interconnected Nissen huts housing the Pantry Dockyard Railway and a workshop stood on one side of a babbling brook which rushed towards the English Channel many feet below. As always, I felt the need to pinch myself to check I wasn't dreaming. Had I really been given charge of a large part of G. P. Keen's famous railway collection, his magnificent pre-war 'K Lines' system, together with drawings, photographs and other associated equipment? And what on earth was I going to do with it?

We continued along the side of the stream, through the long grass, trying to avoid the adders and lizards that basked there. At the second Nissen hut, I found myself staring at a mysterious graded pathway, gated at the boundary of the Keen estate, which led invitingly up the grassy hillside and out of sight. Tracks disappearing into undergrowth always remind me of my childhood spent playing on the abandoned Admiralty Chatenden & Upnor Light Railway, but I set my curiosity aside — I had quite enough on my plate! I needed to keep my mind on the task of clearing the property of the former President of the Model Railway Club and Chairman of Bassett-Lowke.

I later discovered that this grassy path had been cut so that Captain W. F. P. Kelly could walk down the valley from his own purpose-built hut — which contained his Gutland Railway — to visit his lifelong friend Keen. I had begun to suspect that much of what I had found was not the collection of one man but of several, and possibly Keen's wife, Alma, as well. For two years I disregarded this suspicion, along with most of the material I had found on Captain William F. P. Kelly, but now I have returned to the time machine.

Captain Kelly (Bill to his friends) was one of the pioneers of finescale modelling in the United Kingdom, indeed in Western Europe. He built five layouts in all, two during his childhood and three during his adult years. The first of the adult systems was called 'The South Devon Railway' and was built at Exmouth after he settled there following his marriage to Ella in 1923. This was followed by the Gutland Railway which he began about 1935 in a purpose-built

The Remarkable Captain Kelly

Captain William Francis Peek Kelly was well-bred, wealthy and a friend of some of the most famous names in the development of our hobby. His closest associate was G. P. Keen, one of the leading lights in the Model Railway Club, and he served as a director of the pioneering Rocket Precision company with W. S. Norris, Sir Francis Leyland Barrett and Colonel G. G. Templer. He commissioned models from Stanley Beeson, corresponded with the likes of Henry Greenly and J. N. Maskelyne — who addressed him as 'My dear Kelly' — and wafted around the world in fast cars and luxury liners. He contributed massively to Keen's famous 'K Lines' railway as well as creating his own — first the 'South Devon' and then the extraordinary 'Gutland', which abolished the English Channel. In many ways, he was the picture of the well-to-do Englishman who could indulge his railway passion to the full, working at the leading edge and co-opting the best brains and hands to help, even to the extent of commissioning someone to build him a trainload of naked women — the fabled 'Erotic Express'. Yet compared to Keen, whose name is chiselled into the history of the hobby, the secretive Kelly barely made a footnote. MICHAEL SHAW has found out more about an extraordinary man:

Lt. W. F. P. Kelly of the Home Guard, a photo taken at Hythe in 1941.

Capt. Kelly (on the right) displaying a GWR 'Castle' class 4–6–0, scratchbuilt by him for his South Devon Railway, to Sir Francis Leyland Barrett, director of the Great Western Railway. This photograph was taken by a GWR official photographer in 1927.

structure on the hills overlooking the sea at Hythe in Kent where he had recently moved. It remained in place throughout the Second World War even though it was on an exposed hilltop and a clear temptation to German airgunners. In 1958, after Ella's death, it was dismantled, carefully packed and moved to another purpose-built location at a somewhat lower altitude on the Sandgate Road at Hythe. It was only partially rebuilt here because, after a long illness during which he was nursed by his second wife (who had previously cared for his first wife), Bill died of cancer in 1962. The layout was willed to G. P. Keen and fortunately survives. Originally GPK, as Keen was known, offered the whole layout to the Model Railway Club at Keen House, London. 'O' gauge was not the most popular scale in the early 1960s and this huge 38-year-old layout of a foreign prototype built to coarse prewar standards, with power supplied by the third rail, was politely but firmly declined.

Subsequently, a good half of the system's rolling stock did not remain with the layout as originally intended. It was disposed of or retained by Keen with the result that only 39 of the original 80 locomotives ended up in France, where Keen had found a home for the layout. Some of the more exotic and unusual pieces have turned up years later all over the place! As with Keen's stock, I had little trouble tracing its whereabouts either in the United Kingdom and on mainland Europe, although I was rather surprised to find so many grandees of our hobby so embarrassed about their possessions!

Keen employed David Sinclair, a young modeller from the Folkestone, Hythe & District Model Railway Club – which Keen had founded – to pack Kelly's Gutland Railway into two BR containers, each weighing 4 tonnes. These were transported to France where David rebuilt the layout as a continuous circuit at the Museon di Rodo in Uzes under the

watchful eye of Henri Giro Eymery and Jean Falize (fathers of finescale modelling in France). The railway, renamed the GUR-RUG (Gutland Uzetian Railways – Reseau Uzétian de Gutlande), became a sort of O gauge Pendon with a band of friends, including a retired French Admiral, who each took a part in lovingly maintaining and running it as a continuous museum exhibition. The late President of the Gauge O Guild, John Mumford, was one of the GUR-RUG's staunchest supporters and a regular visitor and restorer! After Henri's death a few years ago, the whole layout was moved again, this time to the nearby Musée du Train et du Jouet at Arpaillargues.

The Gutland Railway was built on a point-to-point basis and was prewar finescale ('O' gauge coarse) and fully scenic. It was called the 'Gutland' because of a comment by G. P. Keen that he thought its plan looked like the gut of a mammal. The system was intended to portray a railway on an imaginary island adjoining both the European mainland and the British Isles. It was connected by a rail tunnel to allow the running of German and French international trains. Bill would have loved the Channel Tunnel and Channel Link!

The main station was called 'Anatomopolis'. The layout was fully automated with banks of relays and many hidden sidings, although it could be manually operated if required. Lights at the windows of a fairytale castle told the owner which of the many hidden storage sidings were occupied. Most of the track was laid using brass bullhead rail on timber sleepers which were chaired and keyed in prototypical manner, but some track utilised flat-bottomed German silver rail. The layout was a 24V DC outside third rail system rectified with a 20 amp output. It was fully electrically and mechanically interlocked and signalled, a rarity even on present-day railway layouts. Kelly was a wealthy man, and he needed to be to produce such a layout.

It is remarkable that outside the hallowed portals of Keen House in London (home of the Model Railway Club) and model engineering circles, and except for a few photographs published by G. P. Keen in the old *Model Railway News*, Bill Kelly is virtually unknown to model railway enthusiasts. He was not widely known even during his lifetime, although he was both a director and the driving force behind Rocket Precision and many initiatives at the MRC were instigated by him. Bill was a very good artist/draughtsman, model maker and photographer with a special interest in landscapes and architecture. He was also joint founder with G. P. Keen and Capt. J. P. Howey (RH&DR) of the Folkestone, Hythe & District Model Railway Club. He was well travelled and humorous, if rather stuffy with those he didn't know. He was a retiring personality who I never met, although I once observed him at the Model Engineer Exhibition. In addition, I suspect his wide-ranging interest in models and railways beyond the British Isles limited his appeal to British modellers.

William Francis Peek Kelly was born to wealthy parents, descended from the Irish peerage, on 5th December 1896 at Harrogate, Yorkshire, and had a privileged childhood. He went to public school, joined the Royal Artillery as a subaltern in 1915 at the age of 18 and, after training, was sent to Flanders. He

survived the war without injury and upon returning home went to Clare College, Cambridge. Here, in 1919, he was introduced to the young G. P. Keen, although the latter was not a student contemporary. When required for formalities, Kelly stated his occupation was 'Gentleman' and later 'Company Director'. At the time of his marriage in 1923 he purchased his first home, Brandon, at Exmouth in

South Devon, where he was on good terms with his near neighbour, Sir Francis Leyland Barrett, Lord of Torquay Manor, who was later also to become a director of Rocket Precision. Leyland Barrett was also a very early GWR finescale modeller and leading light in the prewar MRC.

Kelly's first model, the South Devon Railway, was a mixture of GWR and GNR practice that evolved to take on a

Brandon, Exmouth, W. F. P. Kelly's first house and marital home. The South Devon Railway was housed in the single-storey building with pitched roof to the left of the main building.

Another GWR official photograph, showing a selection of Kelly's South Devon stock at the MRC exhibition in 1927.

Four rows of W. F. P. Kelly's stock from the South Devon Railway, at the MRC exhibition at Central Hall, Westminster, in 1929.

Kelly with his Bentley in Snowdonia in 1936. He loved just looking at beautiful landscapes and was photographed here by his wife Ella.

more Continental flavour as the years passed. This was partially due to his experience of the railways of Northern France during the Great War. Kelly travelled widely during the 1920s, '30s, and '50s with his wife, Ella, and often the Keens, Geoffrey and Alma. Both couples seemed to have good connections with people in the USA, France, Switzerland, Austria and Germany. The Kellys were very fond of cruising and went around the world photographing trains on the 1934 World Cruise of the new Canadian Pacific liner, *Empress of Britain*. It visited Egypt, Southern Africa, India, China, Japan, Australia, New Zealand, Canada and the western USA, enabling Bill to take many pictures of railway interest. Bill and Ella returned to England in good time to experience the Battle of Britain raging over their home in Kent, and the

Above: *Kelly (on the left) with G. P. Keen on a lineside photographic trip and picnic at Headcorn in Kent in the summer of 1941. The photograph was taken by Keen's wife Alma.* Right: *SR 'Schools' class 4−4−0 photographed on the same occasion*

Kelly with Alma Keen beside the line at Headcorn, photographed by G. P. Keen.

coastal bombardment that followed the fall of France (whose coast is clearly discernible from Kelly's railway shed). By January 1942, the Kellys were resident with the Keens at Lustleigh in Devon.

During the Second World War, Kelly enlisted as a Lieutenant in the Local Defence Volunteers (LDV – 'Look, Duck and Vanish!') which became the Home Guard in July 1940. His correspondence and photographs from this period show that life was initially little affected by the war. Throughout it all, he took photographs and corresponded regularly with people all over the world, including occupied Europe and, indeed, Nazi Germany itself. Kelly, like Keen, was useful to British Intelligence because of his vast photographic collection showing European locations and transport infrastructure.

There is still much I don't understand about this period of Kelly's life and that of his friend, G. P. Keen. Kelly had moved to Kent in the mid-1930s although he loaned a property he owned in South Devon to the Keens until they, in turn, eventually moved to Lustleigh on the edge of Dartmoor for the duration of the war. As noted earlier, the Kellys also ended up there for the war. It was Kelly

who encouraged the Keens to move to the Sene Valley in Kent, just below his own 'Shepherds Way'. He instigated the formation of the Sene Valley Estate Company in 1945 which exploited the local area's potential but also controlled its development. The company was wound up by Keen in September 1965 after the sale of most of its land holdings.

From the earliest days, Kelly was very much a motoring enthusiast, owning a succession of cars, including a Standard, Rolls-Royce and at least two Bentleys.

He often acted as chauffeur to the Keens because GPK preferred not to drive. He left his much-loved 3.5 litre Bentley, registration HBO 864, to Keen when he died. Geoffrey Keen kept the vehicle until his own death in 1973 and the family did not dispose of it until October 1974 and then only because of its excessive thirst for petrol.

Kelly and Keen both built their own models and commissioned others for themselves and each other, often from the same person. They swapped and

The Gutland Railway shed, at Shepherds Way in 1935, awaiting the fitting of its roof. The partitioned section at the left of the picture comprised an entrance lobby, ventilated workshop and a lavatory.

Kelly's home, Shepherds Way, Hythe, in the snows of winter 1940. The shed which housed the Gutland Railway can be seen on the extreme left of the picture.

Gutland Railway Anatomopolis South box (based on Basle) and the loco yard, photographed in 1955.

Left: *Anatomopolis station, the terminus of the Gutland Railway.* Right: *A view along the embankment from Wayside station. All the details follow French practice of the 1930s.*

A view of the cutting from the tunnel mouth, with the well-modelled culverted river between the tracks.

photographed models on each other's layouts. Kelly would run notional trains purporting to be from Keen's layout on his own to add interest to its operation, and vice-versa. Distinguishing the stock is difficult, but generally Keen's stock was 'K-Lines' green with grey roofs, whilst Kelly's Gutland stock was maroon or red oxide with black roofs. They also swapped photographs and negatives; many Kelly images appear in the Keen family albums. Thirty years on, the level of confusion caused whilst trying to piece all this together can only be imagined! It was further compounded by the 'in' humour that ran between these lifelong friends. Both often acted like schoolboys and were exceedingly secretive. The hilarious (but unpublishable) correspondence between them could form the basis for a very good screenplay, when I have a few generations to spare!

In the early 1930s much of both Keen's and Kelly's stock was built by a brilliant young modelmaker named J. C. Shaw, who was also employed by Bassett-Lowke until his untimely death in 1936. Both owned items by Stanley Beeson who had been given his very first commission for an LNER N2 0–6–2T by Keen. However, the most unusual rolling stock was built

The interior of one of Kelly's Gutland Railway sleeping cars with its 'erotic' passengers.
MICHAEL J. MILLER

by a Frenchman, Marcel Rossi, and took the form of two separate trains of sleeping cars. The first set, belonging to Keen, consisted of six cars and a bogie Fourgon (full parcels brake) of the Compagnie Internationale de Wagons Lits et de Grande Express Européens. It was painted in dark blue with silver roofs and gilt lettering. Nothing too unusual there, but it was filled with nubile young women figures, each perfectly cast in plaster of Paris, all in states of undress and detailed and painted in the style of a girlie magazine. Not to be outdone, Kelly ordered a similar train, this time based on a PLM prototype. It comprised four articulated cars and a full brake, and part is shown here. Kelly and Keen are reported as saying that Marcel Rossi was to blame for these interesting interiors; that was his joke on the two of them. This was

not the case — Marcel kept strictly to his briefs.

Captain Kelly was essentially a private person but, with his friends, G. P. Keen, W. S. Norris, Sir Francis Leyland Barrett, Col. C. W. Tyrell and Col. G. G. Templer (famous for the book *Building Model Locomotives*) — all of them directors of Rocket Precision Limited at one time or another — he was a trail-blazer for finescale model engineering. These men, together with W. J. Bassett-Lowke, played a part in changing the direction of British modelling from the coarseness of the pre-World War I era to something more akin to the scale modelling we see today. Sadly, Kelly's interest in things continental precluded him a place in British modelling history although, in very much the same way as the British railway engineer De Glehn, his work is appreciated the other side of the channel!

Captain Kelly in his 1928 20hp Rolls Royce beside the Great Western main line at Cockwood, Devon, in 1930. The River Exe is the backdrop to the line here and it can be clearly seen in this photograph.

SMALL PRAIRIE

BRIAN WILLIAMS chooses a Malcolm Mitchell kit of the GWR 45XX
as a first exercise in etched kit building:

Many years ago, when 4mm finescale railway modelling was synonymous with K's and Wills locos running on Peco spiked or Jim Russell's 'Little Western' track, I was reasonably content to have built most of the K's range of GWR engines. With more experience came a desire for more details, such as brake blocks, vacuum pipes and lamp irons.

In those far-off days, my annual source of inspiration usually came from the Pendon and HMRS displays at the Model Railway Club Show at Westminster and the Bristol Show at Whiteladies. Then, my expectations were modest and I was easily satisfied. However, the more my interest developed – usually after acquiring another part of the RCTS series on the GWR loco theme – the greater grew my dissatisfaction with the narrow gauge appearance of 16.5mm track.

Being an avid reader of the model railway press, I became aware of the advantages of EM gauge and without any real thought I did what seemed logical at the time and converted. Then having built two locos in EM, the Model Railway Study Group started publishing their articles in *Model Railway Constructor*.

Not only did they arouse my interest – they created a desire for further improvements. I disposed of everything and decided to make a fresh start in P4. On reflection, this may have been a drastic action, as very few components were available. However, with the need to carry out major improvements to my house and the demands of two young children, serious modelling disappeared off the list of priorities anyway, and I joined the ranks of the armchair modellers, South Wales Regiment. A great darkness descended on my modelling activities which was to last for several years.

This article describes my first exercise in building an etched brass loco kit. Prior to my conversion to 18.83mm I had built numerous whitemetal loco kits. Whilst this created increased awareness of scale appearance, I became increasingly dissatisfied with the quality of the kits available. I had managed to build a few sprung chassis, which just served to highlight the deficiencies of the cast superstructure. My encounter with etched kits results from a chance meeting with Malcolm Mitchell at the Bristol Exhibition about seven years

ago. I purchased a set of his etchings for a GWR 45XX. A year or so passed, with the odd fitting being obtained for that proverbial rainy day. But it was boredom with Saturday night TV that eventually led me to build the 45XX. I chose the chassis as the starting point as there are no complex curves to form or awkward soldering to be done.

The previous chassis I had built to 18.83mm gauge were all sprung and the 45XX was to be no exception. This is where things started to go wrong. All the driving wheel axles were fitted with sprung hornblocks, using the appropriate jigs to solder the hornguides onto the side frames as per instructions. For some reason I simply could not get the chassis to run smoothly. This had been my first failure with springing and was probably due to the axle holes not being concentric to the guide faces. This made me seriously reconsider my views on compensation and, with nothing to lose, I decided to give it a try. However, as I had removed all the hornblock cut-outs, I now had to accurately reposition the fixed rear driving wheel hornguides. Using a home-made jig in brass, this allowed the guides

Photos: PHILIP HALL

to be soldered in at the correct distance from the top of the chassis. The remaining hornguides were soldered to the inside of the chassis using jigs and coupling rods to achieve the correct centres. The chassis was then temporarily fitted with Ultrascale wheels and coupling rods. To my delight, it ran like a dream.

For some time, the thought of attempting to bend Malcolm's superb etchings proved too daunting. However, I eventually made a start on the footplate, followed by the tank and bunker base units. At this stage I chose to strengthen the half-etched cross ties on the tank tops with bullhead rail soldered to the underside. These were cut away after the boiler and firebox units were fitted. I felt this temporary strengthening was necessary as there is a tendency for the tanks to collapse inwards when handling the assembly.

The stage had now come when the tankside overlays had to be bent. I felt at the time that if the brass was annealed it would be easier to make small adjustments to the bend if it didn't come out spot-on at the first attempt. This proved to be unnecessary, and if anything a disadvantage, as the area of annealed brass becomes prone to denting due to its softness.

Next I tackled the rear of the coal bunker. With the overlays bent and soldered in position, the top corners of the rear extension were strengthened with pieces of 1½ x 1½mm brass angle soldered inside. A curved inside face was then produced by the use of a round riffler file to match the outside curve which had previously been filed to shape. The top of the bunker was then finished off by soldering the beading in position. Considerable care is needed with the horizontal curves on the bunker as it is one of those very distinctive design features on Churchward tank engines. If they are not exactly right, the appearance of the bunker is spoilt.

Returning to the footplate, the front overlay was bent to shape. Surprisingly, I had trouble with this part, even after annealing, no doubt due to the small radius of the bend where the footplate turns up under the front of the smokebox front. Again, with the firebox, considerable care was taken with the front end to get the characteristic Churchward shape. The taper boiler section held no problems.

I had now reached the stage where I had to come to terms with having to bend the smokebox/boiler wrapper. I had pondered the problem at length, and during one meeting of the Swansea Model Railway Group, someone from the armchair wing suggested the Guy Williams method of preforming the bend. The following week John Spencer presented me with a chunk of rusty metal that purported to be a vee-block. However, its crude appearance belied the ease at which it produced a tube by simply pressing the etched part into the vee with a suitable-sized bar whilst imparting a circular motion. I could now produce a truly concentric boiler. My main fear of etched brass loco construction had disappeared, to be replaced with a vision of the completed engine.

I started to detail the basic superstructure with the riveted strips along the bottom of the tanks and bunker. To say that I experienced difficulty is an understatement. After some considerable time, burnt fingers and much blue air, the task

was finished. Later I was to return to this tiresome problem when part of the bottom strapping on one side broke away. It seems that the long-term effect of acid flux, if not properly removed, is questionable. At this point, I reached an all-time low. However, a phone call to Malcolm Mitchell resulted in him saving the situation with a spare. This was soldered on at the first attempt and I am sure that the problems I initially had in attaching the riveted strips were due to my poor soldering technique and not neutralising the acid flux.

The smokebox saddle proved to be rather awkward as I had been heavy-handed and had broken off one of the end pieces. However, when finally complete with all its simulated bolts, I was well pleased. With the smokebox, I expected the difficult part to be the soldering of the boiler formers to the wrapper because of their relative thinness. Having just purchased a Unimat 3 lathe, I now had a good reason to try it out. Two formers were turned from 1/16in thick brass and soldered into the wrapper. The smokebox, together with the saddle, was then soldered to the footplate and side

tanks, having first attached the motion plate to the footplate. At this stage I sat back and relaxed – I had a superstructure in front of me. Although devoid of all boiler fittings and other appendages, it faithfully exhibited the classic lines of a Churchward small Prairie. This was a tremendous boost to my confidence.

At this point I decided to incorporate as much additional detail as possible. A start was made by replacing the etched protective window bars on the rear of the cab with 5 amp fuse wire, six to each window. This turned out to be a mistake as the chosen engine would represent mid-1920s condition with tall safety valve cover, inside steam pipes and vertical seams to side tanks, thus restricting engines up to 4555. Working only from photographs, I later deduced that from 4555 onwards, six bars were fitted, but below 4555, four or five bars were fitted. I didn't think that it would be possible to redrill the holes in the cab rear to receive the five bars, so I removed it from the cab to use as a template to cut out a new one. This has the bunker doors in the open position to allow the cab interior to be viewed.

The cladding over the insulating material on the firebox of the prototype is made of thin sheet steel in several sections – corner, side and top sections. On the model, because of the limitations

of the etching process, the edges of the overlapping top sheet are represented by raised lines. These were filed off and shaped pieces of .002in thick brass shim soldered on the top of the firebox between the etched securing bands. As this had the effect of reducing the thickness of the bands, new ones were cut from .002in shim and soldered on top of the firebox and part of the way down the sides, thus restoring the thickness of the bands. Care was taken to shape the ends of the new bands where they met the vertical in order to achieve a smooth shape. The bands were finally finished off with 5 amp fuse wire to represent the securing bolts. Brass wire was soldered into holes drilled into the bases of lamp brackets and the strap, which is bent over the boiler and secures the tanks together.

For some time I had been wondering how I would represent the front end stays and their smokebox securing points. I wasn't going to be satisfied with just soldering lengths of .9mm dia wire to the smokebox. Eventually, having experimented with flattening the end of the stay wire – without any success – I cut out two small rectangles of .010in thick brass, drilled them for the wire to simulate the fixing bolts, then a central slot was filed to receive the stay. The rectangles were then curved to suit the smokebox and soldered in place.

A very noticeable feature of GW taper-boilered tank engines is the shaped sheeting that covers the gap between the boiler and the inner tank sides. It's attached to the tank tops and curves in an upward direction onto the boiler/firebox sides, and its function is to prevent the crew from getting their feet trapped when on top of the tanks. The precise size and shape seems to vary considerably, particularly in later years; basically there are three sections per side. These are made from .002in thick brass shim. The size of each section is pure conjecture.

Additional detail on the tank tops comprises nickel silver turnings to represent the timber filler cover stops, their retaining brackets being cut from .004in thick brass. Also two four-feed lubricator boxes are carried – Martin Finney kindly agreed to supply some castings from his superb 28XX kit. The stub pipes were removed and the casting drilled for new pipes, of 5-amp fuse wire, which were superglued in place. The lubricators are supported on small brackets attached to the tank tops. The feed pipes disappear under the sheeting between the boiler and the tank top. In addition to these, three were made for the cab, two for the motion plate and one for the front footplate below the smokebox.

By this time, I had decided that the engine to be modelled would be No. 4551 and the period portrayed would require the fitting of Dean tapered buffers. Alan Gibson's were used but as the bodies are of turned brass there is no representation of the fixing bolts or footsteps. These details were simulated by stubs of brass wire soldered into holes in the flange, and the footsteps by carved blobs of plastic padding. Both vacuum pipes are scratch-built from bits of wire and tube turned on the Unimat, and the steam heating pipes are lost wax castings with the hose-pipes removed.

A lot of time has been devoted to the area of the safety valve. The top feed pipes run along the tank tops over the sheeting and bends up to the safety valves. This section is covered with U-shaped pressings made from .022in thick brass. The brass was first bent tightly into shape around the same wire which was to form the clack valves. The lot was flooded with solder, to allow the brass to be filed back to the wire, which was then bent to the boiler radius. Once this has been done, the wire can be removed and the casing fitted over the delivery pipes. Two pieces of the same

thin brass sheet were soldered onto the sides of the safety valve to represent the base flanges of the casings which cover the clack valves.

The safety valve started off as a Spring-side casting. However, as it refused to seat itself properly on the boiler, I ended up using a brass casting from Malcolm's 44XX kit, modified by drilling out the centre so that the whitemetal spring castings could be used. I think the improvement is worth the effort.

Originally I had fitted a cast 44XX chimney, the base of which didn't look right — the work on the safety valve only served to accentuate its thickness. When I bought the etchings, I purchased a Westward chimney but had rejected it because of its overthick rim. I decided that if it could be made to sit properly on the smokebox, it would be an improve-ment on the cast one. It was annealed and the base tweaked to improve its sit. All that it needed now was an improved rim profile, achieved by mounting the chimney on an accurately machined

mandrel. This ensured that when the rim was reprofiled it remained concentric to the base. The eight fixing bolts on the chimney are represented by brass wire soldered into holes drilled after the chimney was glued in place.

The time had arrived to tackle the cylinders and slidebars. As I had already decided to include as much detail as possible, I felt I should attempt to make the valve spindles move. Another and more important reason for this decision was that I had already damaged one of the etched links which connect to the valve rod. I turned the relief valves and piston valve ends from nickel silver and brass rod as per Guy Williams and described in his book *The 4mm Engine*. Before fitting the slidebars, the non-working horizontal faces were filed to the characteristic tapered profile of the GWR two-cylinder engine; the three lubricator cups on each top slidebar were simulated with shaped pieces of nickel silver rather than wire as the lubricators are more

rectangular than circular in plan. On later examination of 4566, I discovered that all three are different.

Construction of the crosshead followed the instructions except that I substituted turned nickel silver shouldered ends and piston rods for the steel and brass tube. Minor improvements involved soldering slivers of nickel silver to the outside of the sliding faces; the etched representation seemed too fine and not like the chunky prototype. I also soldered short lengths of hypodermic tube into the centre of the crosshead to simulate the bearing for the pin attaching the connecting rod. With the crosshead/connecting rods complete, fitting them to the cylinders proved to be an upsetting experience, as on rotating the driving wheels, the crosshead overshot the slidebar ends at maximum stroke by approximately 1½mm. As the cylinder assembly could not be repositioned any further to the rear of the chassis, it appeared that the slidebars were too short. Checking with photographs and drawings confirmed my fears. As to why this should happen, I was probably over-zealous with the file, removing too much off the ends of the slidebars when cleaning them up after soldering them together. Not wanting to strip everything down and start again, I decided to take the easy option and solder pieces of 1/16in thick nickel silver onto the ends of the slidebars and then file to shape. This has worked quite well and the joint is only noticeable on close inspection.

The motion linkage on the ends of the valve rods is turned and fabricated from nickel silver. Whilst the final appearance is very rewarding, one has a tendency to become cross-eyed when making these parts. The linkage is suspended from a tube running over a wire frame which in turn is soldered to the support carrying the cylinders and the slidebar supports, and is hidden from view behind the footplate valance. Whilst I get considerable satisfaction from watching the movement of the linkage, it can only really be viewed from track level, so the amount of extra work required may deter me from incorporating this feature in future projects.

I discarded the cast vacuum pump and replaced it with a fabricated one consisting of 14 parts.

Having decided to represent the engine in mid-1920s condition dictated the use of double brake hangers and the fitting of

pull rods on both sides of the engine rather than the one central arrangement provided in the etch. Although double hangers are provided, they need to be positioned either side of a packing piece. This was achieved by filing scraps of 0.012in thick brass to shape and soldering between the hangers. Brass wire was then passed through the hangers and pull rods and soldered in position. The vertical shaft below the brake standard on the left-hand side of the chassis is made by filing square a short length of small-bore brass tube, into which is soldered wire, which in turn is attached to the brake lever on the chassis. The other end of the wire is bent through 90 degrees and soldered to the top of the chassis.

The driving wheel balance weights are of a very substantial nature and have a bevelled edge to the circumference. Two discs were turned from brass bar to fit inside the tyres. Three balance weights

were then cut from each disc, and similar shaped weights were cut from .005in thick brass sheet to fit the rear of each driving wheel.

The cab interior consists of the parts from the 44XX kit with additional detail. As I have little knowledge of the changes made to the cab over the years, all I can say is that it is as accurate as I can make it with the information available to me. In addition to the lubricator boxes already mentioned, various bits and pieces are fitted – tank water level gauge, turned injector handles, reversing lever, working seats and pipework. The whole lot is finished off with wood facing to tank tops and reversing lever quadrant. The wood is actually 0.6mm thick mahogany veneer which is a very good match to that in 4566.

There are several features of 4551 I am not too happy about. The thing that annoys me the most is the paint finish.

After cleaning, grey cellulose primer was airbrushed on with no problems. Then a green base coat was applied. This was a total disaster as the paint appeared to have dried on contact and had the appearance of coloured talcum powder. I considered stripping the paint off the body but decided against it as I felt more harm than good would result, particularly to the smaller parts. I decided to use T-cut paint polish on as much of the body as possible, using cotton wool swabs. This seemed to be successful but it was impossible to remove the talc effect from the more inaccessible places. The body is finished in Railmatch pre-1927 green as Malcolm Mitchell's wasn't then available.

4551 is the first loco I have attempted to weather. My aim was to try and achieve the appearance of a loco that has seen considerable service since its last repaint but had been well maintained and regularly cleaned. This meant that the brilliance of lettering had to be toned down without obliteration and also that the density of the black areas had to be reduced in addition. I decided that the crew had taken it upon themselves to ignore Swindon practice and polish the safety valve cover and cab porthole window frames. However, it was necessary for the appearance of these parts to be consistent with the condition of the rest of the engine.

The weathering process turned out to be easier than I had expected after a fellow club member passed on a tip used by the plastic aircraft modellers. This requires the following concoction to be sprayed onto the model: 25% enamel thinners, 25% cellulose thinners, 25% Humbrol satin varnish and 25% matt polyurathene varnish. Into this mixture is added, according to the degree of weathering required, small quantities of dark earth and black. This mixture was blown over the model until the desired effect was achieved. When spraying below the footplate, the content of dark earth was increased to give the appearance of oil/grease. I would advise that this operation is only carried out in a well-ventilated room and a face mask is used, as no doubt the mixture is harmful.

Finally, I would like to thank Malcolm Mitchell, not just for producing such an excellent product and thereby making this article possible, but also for putting up with my pestering for one reason or another.

POSTSCRIPT

Since writing this article, the dreaded event has happened — additional information has come to light. Recently, while rummaging through the cheap railway books in a Carmarthen bookshop, I picked up a copy of *Working Yeovil to Taunton Steam* and there was a photograph of 4551 taken in BR days. I immediately purchased the book for the princely sum of £1.

Later, on closer inspection of the photograph, I was dismayed to find that 4551 still retained the early style of rainstrip on the cab roof and flanged air vents on the tank tops. It may be that both tanks and cab roofs moved from engine to engine in the same way as boilers and wheels during overhauls. If this proves not to have been the case, then 4551 will have to live with its inaccuracies until the upheaval of a recent house move and the ensuing rebuilding has been completed - yet more years in the modelling wilderness!

SHOCK TACTICS

No, it's not April 1st. JAS MILLHAM really has built a wobbling shock-absorbing van in S-scale:

There were two vans I wanted to build — a Shockvan and an LNER plywood type. Then I obtained a copy of Geoff Gamble's *British Railway Vans* and, sure enough, plate 55 showed a Diag. 1/201, Lot 2045, shock-absorbing van with LNER-style plywood body. Fifty were built, B850050–B850099, in 1948. When I looked up the Lot No. in Don Rowland's book *British Railways Wagons*, I found it contained a dimensioned diagram of this very vehicle!

Shock-absorbing vehicles — there were wagons as well as vans — were introduced to reduce damage to fragile cargoes during shunting. Biscuits, glass bottles and jars, empty or full, were typical loads. The body was mounted on a subframe which could slide longitudinally on the underframe, restrained by springs on the solebars on both sides of the wagon. If a moving shockvan struck buffer stops or a cut of stationary wagons, not only did the buffer springs compress but the body slid along the underframe until checked by the side springs. As these decompressed, the body returned to its original position and invariably overshot, shimmying about the mid-position until the energy was spent. Since the buffer springs also decompressed, giving the underframe a kick while this was going on, the resulting antics could be quite amusing. Empty, the underframe weighed about twice as much as the body, but fully-loaded the position was reversed and could result in the body wagging the underframe, causing the wagon to roll in a series of jerks! Shockvans were identified by three vertical white stripes (later white squares) on the sides and ends, and were almost invariably vacuum-fitted. They were not, as some people seem to think, barrier wagons to isolate others from the rest of the train — the vulnerable cargo was carried in the shock absorbing wagon itself.

Construction of my S-scale model commenced with the modification of some old

I didn't notice until after the photos had been taken that I'd missed off the door catch and grab handle. This has since been rectified.

(a) Pendulum bob. (b) Solder tag to take one end of motion transfer link. (c) 'V' groove and ball bearings. (d) Body 'anchor' for other end of motion transfer link. (e) Nuts soldered to chassis to take body retaining screws.

ERG loco buffers into heavy-duty wagon buffers by soldering 6BA washers to the heads and turning them down to size. Brass channel solebars and headstocks were soldered to a sheet brass floor and MJT S-scale W-irons added. These were not quite correct for this baby, so I modified them with a backing strip, filled the front with solder, filed it flush and drilled holes to represent the plate type. A rectangle was cut out of the floor in between the W-irons and an A-frame of 20-thou brass erected with pinpoint bearings for the pendulum, which was made from a bit of ⅝in brass rod drilled and tapped 6BA and mounted on a length of 6BA studding. A

solder tag located by two nuts was fitted between the bob of the pendulum and the pivot to attach the link for transferring the motion to the body.

The body itself was made of plastic card and Plastruct sections. In order to make the body move freely enough on the chassis, pieces of 2mm brass angle were soldered to the floor to form V-grooves. The body was placed in position on bits of 15-thou plastic card to space it off the floor and secured with Blu-tack. Two ⅛in ball-bearings were placed in each V-groove and held with more Blu-tack, which also held in place corresponding pieces of Plastruct angle on top of the

Continued on page 66

The Lineside Sailing Barge

Places at which the railways and shipping interconnect have long exerted a fascination for modellers, offering operational opportunities and scenic challenges. Never one to shirk a challenge, DAVE ROWE designed the famous 4mm diorama 'Exebridge Quay' knowing that he would have to populate the wet bits with suitable vessels. The result of his labours
– as exemplified by the barge described here – was a spectacular adjunct to the railway proper:

From childhood, we are all indoctrinated with the fallacious historical information that the wheel was early man's greatest invention and that its introduction changed the world. Of course, in reality the wheel had little impact until the early 19th century when men, at last, were able to provide a smooth hard surface for it to run on — iron rails. It was actually the ship which allowed the first bulk transport of men and materials across seas and along rivers for the purposes of war or trade, thereby greatly affecting history; the growth of such cities as London, Bristol, York and Plymouth, for example, had more to do with shipping than railways. It is perhaps for this reason that in my quest for new challenges to stretch my modelling abilities, the idea of a dock scene had been gestating for some years before the Exebridge diorama was started. From time to time I had seen vessels on layouts, but I cannot recall any that looked right. I didn't know anything about ships but was perfectly capable of

recognising that some showed unrealistically coarse, hairy rigging whilst others, when compared with the 4mm figures set around them, appeared to be in a different scale to the rest of the layout. My lack of certain knowledge stilled these critical thoughts and instead induced apprehension; how would I, in my turn, cope when it came to constructing such vessels for a diorama portraying the 1840s?

The possibility of anything ready-made was quickly eliminated, for most were garish polythene things suitable only for the bath-tub. I next turned to commercial kits and found that the Danish 'Billing Boats' range, stocked by many model shops, covered several scales and various eras. Their list showed two kits at 7mm scale, seven at 4mm and four at 3mm with a wide selection of models in some ten other scales. There was, of course, a catch — the two 7mm vessels, for example, were an ultra-modern luxury yacht and Professor Cousteau's research vessel *Calypso*, complete with bright

yellow plastic bathyscaph. Similarly, the 4mm kits were quickly whittled down: two were of 17th century vessels, one was American and another represented an ultra-modern Dutch tug. This left three kits — the auxiliary steam-assisted sailing vessel *Danmark*, the *Cutty Sark* and a Dutch sailing barge. The *Cutty Sark* and the *Danmark* were ruled out since vessels of their size would not have traded from small West Country docks, while the Dutch sailing barge was quite different in character to the English version; it was also labelled 'suitable for beginners' and, whilst I truly fitted that bill, the photograph showed a somewhat toy-like model, bereft of detail. Another unpromising factor was the basic nature of the Billings kits, which come in two parts — the wood and other materials necessary to produce a vessel 'body' and a second kit of fittings (portholes, winches etc.) which can cost more than the 'body' kit and contain items in plastic, wood or brass; some, such as the winches, are beautifully turned and have prices to match. From the catalogue it appears that fittings are produced in two, three or four sizes and each kit is allocated parts which are to the nearest available scale — three sizes of fittings for a total of 13 scales is a far cry from the accuracy expected by railway modellers.

A second point, of course, is the sheer size of ships. The largest sailing vessel ever built would, in 4mm scale, be 6ft 8in long and over 3ft high! Even the *Cutty Sark*, a swift midget, would be 43 inches long. Early on in my research for the diorama I found that neither of the two docks on which it is based (Exeter and Bridgewater) could admit vessels over 110ft in length and that most of the ships using them were coastal traders — mainly ketches and schooners in the period to be portrayed. To stay within these limits it was clearly going to be necessary to scratchbuild whatever I needed, but a book which was recommended to me as helpful (*West Country Coasting Ketches* by Slade and Greenhill) contained totally incomprehensible passages with up to three unknown technical terms in each line. So I moved on to catalogues of drawings from David MacGregor Plans and Bassett Lowke Ltd. The scales vary according to the size of the prototype, as it seems that ship modellers prefer to end up with something between 30 and 40 inches long. I worked out the sizes of the prototypes, ruling out two thirds as being too large and half the remainder as unsuitable types.

This still left a good selection, and of these I decided that a ketch, a schooner, a barquentine and a sailing barge would give an interesting assortment in the diorama whilst the varied styles would maintain interest during the many months their construction would take. All very well, but how does one start? At the South Wales Model Show at Bridgend I found several expert modellers demonstrating the scratchbuilding of ships but these worthies had been so many years in the hobby that they seemed to have forgotten their tentative steps and insisted that one could easily carve hulls from solid blocks of timber; my common sense insisted the opposite. At the same show I saw a kit by Artesania Latina (of Spanish manufacture) of the schooner *Scottish Maid*, built in 1839. It was to scale of 1:50 and consequently of no use for the diorama but I decided it would be excellent tuition in ship building and the comprehensive plans could be photocopied down to 4mm scale so that the same craft could be constructed again in the smaller scale using plastic instead of wood. For most keen ship modellers who scratchbuild sailing vessels, styrene would not be regarded as an appropriate modelling medium; acceptable for a World War II battleship perhaps but, for the purist, wood is the only material for a sailing barge or schooner. Those to whom I mentioned plastic either refused to even consider the idea or walked away, sadly shaking their heads at this poor misguided character's strange ideas,

yet it seemed to me that a material with which I had become familiar as a result of using it extensively for 15 years was clearly a sensible one to employ and the need for the models to sit in real water for up to a week at a time clinched the matter. Wood has other minor drawbacks — a tendency to split, grain which needs filling, rough ends on cross grain cuts and, where left unpainted, the grain is, of course, 76 times over scale.

The wood kit assembly went well and was a most pleasant exercise. Even in this small ship there were over a thousand components so the project consumed many hours, but the superb drawings needed little written explanation as every part was numbered in the sequence in which it had to be installed; this helped boost my confidence for tackling it in plastic. The 4mm version of the schooner eventually went well, as it should have done being only a simple reduction exercise, although items such as the small rigging fittings, which came preformed in the wooden kit, needed techniques to be devised for their speedy mass production.

Moving on to the barge required another big step — from mere copying in a smaller scale to working fresh from drawings. Obviously, as a novice, one couldn't just launch straight in, so during the two years prior to the start of construction I had been reading avidly all the books on ships and ship modelling that the local library could supply, rather a lean selection when compared with the vast range

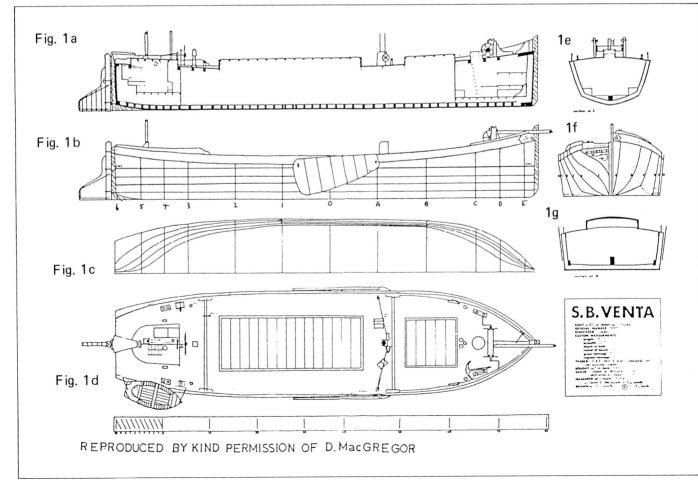

Fig. 1a

Fig. 1b

Fig. 1c

Fig. 1d

1e

1f

1g

S.B. VENTA

REPRODUCED BY KIND PERMISSION OF D. MacGREGOR

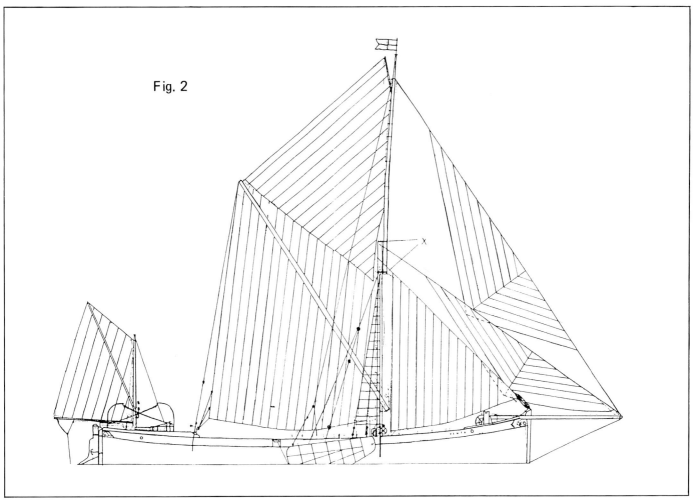

Fig. 2

dealing with railways and I also discovered that, with the exception of sailing barges, there is a dearth of preserved vessels, especially wooden ones. Locomotives may look large, but when one visits Greenwich and sees the masts of *Cutty Sark* towering above the tall adjacent buildings, the costs and space requirements of preservation become apparent. Some of the warehouses modelled in 'Exebridge Quay' house the Exeter Maritime Museum but as their collection is global in coverage, there is little of British origin. On the other hand, the Historic Ships Collection at St Katherine's Dock, Tower Bridge, London, is all British and the National Maritime Museum at Greenwich has superb models. Yes, I know that for some of you there is no world outside railways, but my intended one hour visit to St Katherine's turned into a whole afternoon and the two hours intended at Greenwich became a full day. Naturally the Science Museum has many excellent models and I found a few more at the Maritime Museum in Southampton. The St Katherine's Collection includes a three-masted topsail schooner *Kathleen & May* plus the Thames sailing barge *Cambria* and usually a good number of privately-owned sailing barges are kept in the same dock. *Cambria* traded as far as Exeter so there was justification for having a sailing barge in the diorama while *Kathleen & May* regularly plied the Irish Sea

and the English Channel. Drawings were available for *Kathleen & May* but not for *Cambria* so I purchased plans of a sailing barge *Venta* while extensively photographing *Cambria*. The latter, incidentally, is thought to be the very last vessel trading around Britain's coast exclusively under sail, not ceasing to ply until 1971. Such vessels are usually called Thames barges but the fact that *Cambria* traded as far as Exeter shows that they were far from being confined to the Thames; whilst ketches and schooners might have been the most commonly seen vessels trading around the west coast of Britain, these barges dominated the east coast from Lincolnshire to Dorset, sometimes even calling at French ports.

These flat-bottomed vessels, numbering around 2,000 at the turn of the century, were able to penetrate far inland into shallow waters while carrying heavy loads; to do this they could not have deep keels, having instead two triangular lee boards, one either side, which could be winched up to give a shallow draught (*Fig. 2*). The other feature which allowed them to get inland was their ability to lower masts while under way, with the sails set, so that low bridges were no obstacle. With a crew of just two, pretty nifty work was required at such times as I presume that lowering the mast had to be left until the last moment in order not to lose momentum, then speedily

raised after the bridge was passed; for stretches such as Tower Bridge to Putney, with fifteen bridges in seven miles, special low-bridge sails were used. *Cambria* was unusual in trading to such a late date without ever having an auxiliary engine fitted and it is a true Thames barge (while *Venta* has the more pointed bow of an East Anglian barge).

THE BARGE MODEL

This description is my method of construction in plastic, with some detail work in brass and using wood for masts etc. If you have woodworking skills there is no reason why you should not carve a hull from a block of solid pine or from a multi-layer sandwich of timbers glued together. Although I wouldn't do it, you could combine a wooden hull and a layout employing real water if you could guarantee a perfect seal; you will also realise when reading through that, even when not using a solid hull, wood could be substituted for plastic in most instances (but you may be appalled at the prices asked for the thin strips of hardwood needed for planking etc).

I worked from the MacGregor plans, photographs and an excellent book on modelling Thames barges. All are essential if you are ever intent on barge making; here, however, I will confine myself to the basic principles and elaborate only where I used what are, for con-

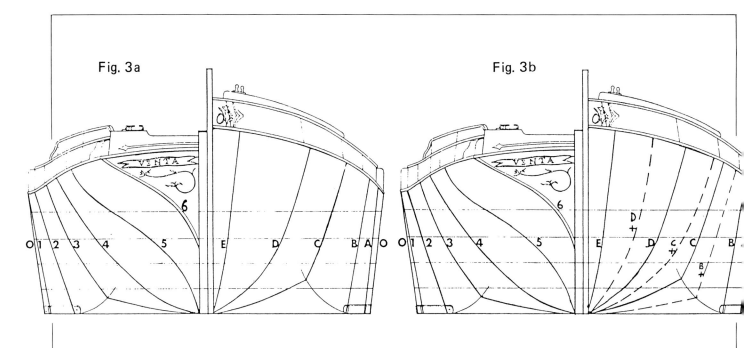

Fig. 3a

Fig. 3b

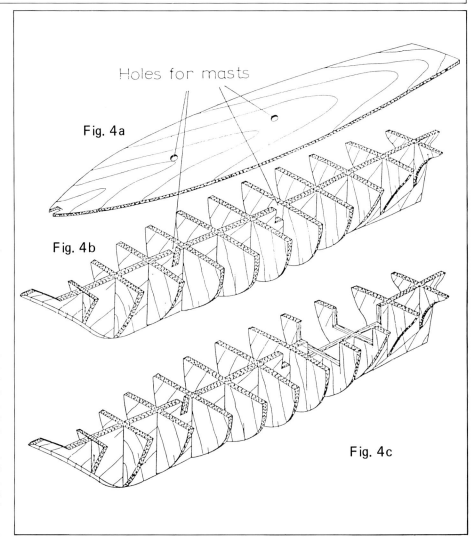

Holes for masts

Fig. 4a

Fig. 4b

Fig. 4c

ventional ship modellers, non-conformist materials and methods. Problems arose at times, so explanations of the means whereby I overcame inexperience are noted.

Often the drawings come as three separate sheets — 'Lines, for scale model', 'Elevation, details and deck plan' and 'Sail and rigging plan' but those for *Venta* came as only two sheets. *Figs. 1 & 2* show a much reduced version of the plans used to model the barge, although in the reduction (to 10% of the original size) much of the fine detail has been lost. The crucial parts for the production of the hull are the ship lines in *1B* and *1F*, the latter being shown to a larger scale in *Fig. 3a*. It will be seen that the lettered and numbered lines on the hull in *Fig. 3a*, which are called sections, are transverse slices through the hull at positions indicated by the corresponding letters and numbers on the elevation *1b*. One half of *Fig. 3a* — the left side — represents the forward part of the ship and the right side represents the after part with the amidships section '0' appearing on both sides.

In my 'trial run' wooden kit all these sections had been pre-cut from plywood and formed into a series of what I will refer to as 'bulkheads' fitted by means of halved joints into the longitudinal 'keel' piece (*Fig. 4b*). As pre-cut pieces they did not appear individually on the scale drawings so I laid them on the photocopier with black paper behind them and reduced down to 4mm scale. The barge drawing shows the twelve sections superimposed, so this time I copied *3a* twelve times, folded each copy down the middle line (print outwards) and cut out each of the twelve sections in turn, opened them out flat and glued them to 3mm styrene, making sure each one was clearly identified. The sections in *3a* only show the shape of the hull — they do not indicate where bulkheads have to be. In the model it was decided that 0, 1, 2, 3, 4, 5, 6, A and B were satisfactory but that at the bow (front) end the marked differences between B, C, D, and E merited intermediate bulkheads halfway between each adjacent pair so B+, C+ and D+ were inserted (*Fig. 3b*) shown as broken lines on the drawing to help keep the lines smooth). If you want to have the hatch covers off you will need to modify the area involved by removing part of the bulkheads and keel as in *Fig. 4c*.

Ship modellers either produce a full hull or model down to the waterline only if they want it set in a 'sea'. In spite of using real water I opted for just-below-the-waterline models as full hulls would have required a deep dock and very large quantities of water. The barge was the exception to this, for its prototypical flat bottom gave just the depth required. Some modellers constructing a ship such as a ketch might want all the hull visible as the vessel lies on the mud in a drained tidal creek but if set in 'water' it could be cut off anywhere between X and Y on *Fig. 5* depending on the degree of loading. What should not be seen is a vessel fully laden with coal apparently floating high in the water!

While it is not difficult to cut the outlines of these 'bulkheads', cutting the slot for the halved joint is tricky. You can't do it with a craft knife but it would be possible using a fret saw and then a file to smooth off the consequent unevenness. I am fortunate in having a Minicraft table saw and for jobs like this it is invaluable. At one time I would have regarded such a small circular saw as a toy but provided one can supply it with 18 volts at up to five amps it can be a real boon. In the past I experienced problems with styrene degradation (*MRJ* Nos. 8 and 9) so, although 3mm styrene may seem a bit excessive, I opted for thickness and safety.

The halved joints along the length of the 'keel' make the assembly rather flexible but as soon as a 1.5mm styrene sheet, cut to the deck shape (*Fig. 4A*) is fixed in place, everything becomes rigid and the planking of the hull can be considered. If you feel capable of carving a solid hull the sections of *Fig. 3a* are used in the opposite way to the 'bulkhead' method. Each of the twelve sections is glued to strong card and the 'bulkhead' part is cut out leaving an external template to hold against the outside of the hull at the appropriate position.

You will see that the deck is curved (or sheared) fore and aft (*Fig. 1a*) as well as being cambered — i.e. higher in the centre (*Fig. 1e*) — so it is necessary to hold it firmly in place with very strong rubber bands which force it into shape while the cement sets or the solvent dries.

The edges of sections B+, C, C+, D, D+, E and 3, 4, 5, 6 needed chamfering (*Fig. 6a*) to give a smooth seating for the planking. There is a tendency for thin styrene planks (.75mm) to soften slightly at each bulkhead due to the action of the solvent or cement, so it was found necessary to use 1.5mm thick strips to ensure smooth lines. One can sit and hold these planks for some time before the solvent dries

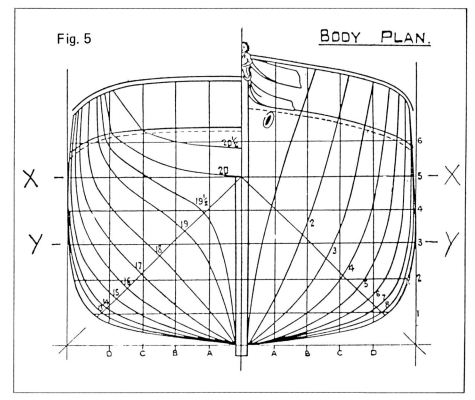

enough to fix them securely but the simple expedient previously of curving the ends of the strips between finger and thumb to something close to the shape required can cut down the holding time by 75%.

On the barge there are very low bulwarks (*Fig. 1e*) (sides of the vessel above deck level) and these were formed from 1mm styrene with a capping rail of the same thickness. On a vessel such as a ketch or schooner the bulwarks are much higher (3ft 6in) with the planking of the hull continued up to this height and supporting timbers visible on the inside. The easiest way to achieve this is to have an inner 1mm styrene core to which planks can be glued on the outside and supporting ribs on the inside (*Fig. 6b*). Planking should start at the top and work downwards with the planks tapered slightly at each end where the vessel narrows. The long non-prototypical 'keel' comes into its own here

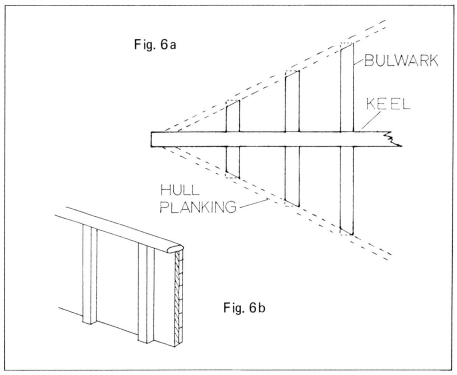

for it protrudes beyond the planked hull to form the 'stem' and 'sternpost' which are shown hatched in *1a* and *1b*. The tapering of the planks has to be judged by eye and I found it useful to hold as many as ten strips in place with my fingers before thinking about gluing them; this gave me a chance to see if the tapering was sufficient. The horizontal lines on the hull in *Fig. 1b* do not indicate planking runs, they are the 'waterlines' and appear again as curved lines in *1c*. It will be seen from *Fig. 3a* that planks which are laid nearly vertically on edge at the section '0' will have been twisted through about 50° by the time they reach section 6 of the stern. With wooden planking this is achieved by steaming the strips and holding them to shape while they cool but styrene planks can be formed to shape while cold by twisting them with the fingers.

When carving a hull from solid timber it is necessary to cut five templates to each of the five outlines in *1c* and check your carving by holding them against the hull at the respective levels indicated in *1b*. The amount of taper on the hull planks needs to be more on a conventional keeled hull and I am afraid that it is not possible to side-step this task by using a flat sheet of scribed styrene, pushed into the complex shape of the hull without losing the characteristic lines of the vessels. For the deck planking, Slater's embossed sheet with 2mm spacing was ideal but obviously there could not be planks in 70ft unbroken runs, so staggered joints were scribed to give 15ft lengths and this was stuck on to the earlier 1.5mm plain deck.

The coamings (sides) to the hatches (access holes to below decks) were cut from 0.75mm styrene and needed an internal ledge to support the hatch covers as well as some means of holding a tarpaulin down over the whole hatch. In earlier days this was achieved by lashings — taking ropes around the coamings while other ropes, fastened to ringbolts on the deck, were taken across the hatch. A later development was to have iron cleats to take steel battens which were wedged against the tarpaulin (*Fig. 7*). The double curvature of the deck needed to be taken into account when forming the hatch coamings and I managed a snug fit to the deck by a process of trial-and-error. Each hatch cover is curved to the same camber as the deck and needs some means of lifting — either handholds or lifting rings. The latter can be individual links from fine chain.

The lee-boards (the triangular boards on either side of the vessel) are not optional extras — all barges use them. They need a pivot at the narrow end and an anchoring point at the other to affix the rope used for raising them. A combination of scribed 2.0mm styrene with microstrip added for the fine detail served both here and for the rudder.

The cabin top was assembled with clear styrene to represent the small glazed areas. The scuttle (access doorway to cabin) was another simple styrene assembly and once these items of deck woodwork were glued in place, attention could be turned to the deck fittings, the most prominent of which is the windlass,

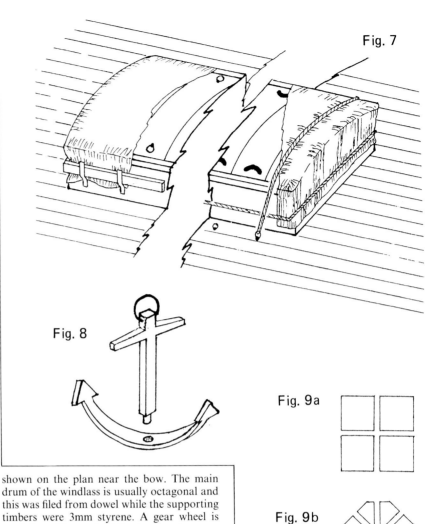

Fig. 7

Fig. 8

Fig. 9a

Fig. 9b

shown on the plan near the bow. The main drum of the windlass is usually octagonal and this was filed from dowel while the supporting timbers were 3mm styrene. A gear wheel is carried at either end of the drum and corresponding pinions are mounted on a shaft with squared ends for the handle which is used when raising the anchor. Gear wheels of 11mm diameter and their pinions are not items I would want to scratchbuild so I visited a member of a profession fast becoming extinct — a watch repairer. He had a big box containing thousands of watch and clock gears and allowed me to help myself to a large selection. A watch gear only 11mm in diameter can be rather thin and, although suitable for a small winch was too frail to represent the gear wheel on the larger windlass. To 'beef them up' I soldered pairs of identical gears together, making sure there was no excess solder to clog the teeth. Various small winches were required and the originals had cast iron frames which, for the model version, were cut from brass sheet with a piercing saw (first sweating two sheets of brass together to obtain identical sides). The spacing bars, shafts and handles were various diameters of brass wire and, although very fiddly, I found them satisfying to make.

The production of an anchor caused some head scratching until I tried the unlikely medium of sheet lead. It could have been filed up from a thick piece of brass or possibly assembled from pieces of styrene (*Fig. 8*) but the lead was easy to cut and bend and half an hour's work produced a couple of acceptable anchors.

My attempts to make the ship's wheel were not so straightforward. These are usually wooden, and brass seemed to be the most appropriate material for the model version — I could turn the hub and have brass wire for the spokes. For the rim it should, I thought, be possible to drill a suitable hole in a thick sheet of brass and then cut out the rim; while attempting to file it round, I managed to buckle my first effort while the second try ended up with unevenly spaced spokes, as did the third. By this time many hours had gone by and I decided to admit defeat and visited the Maritime Models shop at Greenwich to purchase a selection of wheels for the various ships to be made. This was annoying for, at the outset, I had accepted that only chain would have to be purchased, then I had compromised by using watch gears for the winches and now there would be a third item not scratchbuilt. The shop settled the matter for me, however — ship modellers usually scratch build to ¼ in = 1 foot (6mm) or ⅛in—1 foot (3mm) so wheels of a suitable size were not available — I would have to make them myself after all. A different technique was used for the next attempt. Two pieces of brass tube, one just large enough to slide over the other, were soldered together to give a wall thickness suitable for a wheel rim. The double thickness gave enough strength for turning the rim on a lathe and, before parting off, a very small groove was turned in the edge to give a good location for drilling the spoke holes. This technique produced the rims for five wheels in an hour but the means of accurately drilling eight equidistant holes into a hub eluded me for, where an error of 0.5mm in the position of the spoke holes around the circumference of the rim was acceptable, the same error at the hub, with the spokes all in close proximity, shrieked 'mistake'. When round section brass was abandoned in favour of square, hub production improved for it was obviously easy to drill holes for the first four spokes (*Fig. 9a*) and, by filing flats on the corners, the next four holes were drilled (*Fig. 9b*). The holes for all five hubs were drilled and then the rod was turned down to size and parted off. I have since acquired a better lathe and would nowadays locate the holes by using the gears to index the chuck position with the drill mounted vertically on the cross slide.

MASTS, SPARS AND RIGGING
Masts are the vertical timbers from which spars (horizontal or angled timbers) are swivelled. Apparently, by using dowel rod for these items, I committed a sin — degame, spruce or obechi are the recommended timbers to employ. I must admit that my first attempts to taper the dowel rod on a lathe ended in splintered disasters. A more controllable method was simply to file the tapered shape, first filing the thin end down to square section, then hexagonal and finally round with hardly a mishap en route. It will be seen that the main mast is in two section (*Fig. 2*) and two pieces of 3mm sheet brass (X on *Fig. 2*) were drilled with two holes each, and a little Superglue run under the brass gave a firm join here. *Fig. 2* shows a prominent spar at about 50° to the horizontal. This is the 'sprit' from which the correct title for such vessels is derived — spritsail sailing barges. The sprit is tapered at both ends and is supported at its lower end by two short lengths of chain.

When, on a ship, it is necessary to attach ropes or other fittings to a mast or spar, a steel band with eyelets is fitted. Eyelets can be shaped from brass wire or are available ready formed, and I found it best to drill right through the mast and brass band which gave two points for the eyelet wire to be soldered (*Fig. 10a*). When a single fixing point was attempted there was a tendency for the eyelet to come adrift (*Fig. 10b*) or for the whole band to slip.

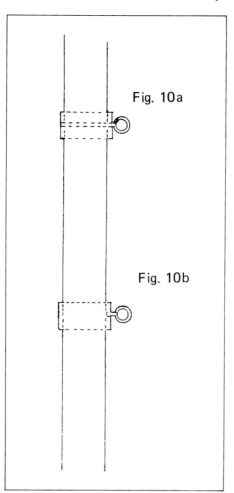

Fig. 10a

Fig. 10b

The rigging of any sailing ship is divided into two categories — standing and running. Standing rigging is the means whereby the masts are supported — on early vessels it would have been tarred hempen ropes but towards the end of commercial sail they tended to be replaced by galvanised wire rope and all later barges have this version. Running rigging is used to raise, lower and control the sails and spars. On most vessels this was of untarred hemp but barges use flexible steel wire rope. The main mast has three supporting ropes (shrouds) each side — these are the ones with rungs (ratlines) shown in *Fig. 2*. At their lower ends the shrouds are attached to the pairs of wooden blocks (deadeyes) and, via these, to the sides of the hull (*Fig. 11*). It would be incorrect to miss out the deadeyes and their connecting rope (lanyard) but although only twelve deadeyes are needed for a barge, my barquentine needed 60, so a simple mass-production technique was devised (although they are available from model shops). I made a small lathe tool to the form shown in *Fig. 12* and this quickly gave the shape of each deadeye's periphery while experiment showed that a piercing saw was the best tool for parting off. Drilling the three holes accurately was achieved by a simple jig — a two-inch hinge — with a suitably sized hole drilled in one leaf and three small holes in the other (*Fig. 13*). The small holes were countersunk to speed up drill location and the dowel-rod-to-deadeye time came down to 30 seconds or less.

A heavy wire (the forestay) runs from the overlapped section of the mainmast down towards the foremost timber of the hull (stem). Two massive three-sheaved iron blocks are set

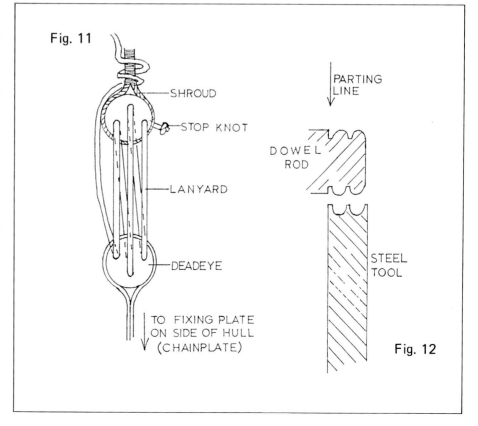

Fig. 11

SHROUD

STOP KNOT

LANYARD

DEADEYE

TO FIXING PLATE ON SIDE OF HULL (CHAINPLATE)

PARTING LINE

DOWEL ROD

STEEL TOOL

Fig. 12

at the lower end of the forestay and these were made from brass on the model. Three slices of rod between four plates equals one block (*Fig. 14*) but little of this block detail can now be seen with the vessel in place in the diorama. The small mast (mizzen) at the rear is similar to the main mast in most ways and the plans indicate where all the standing rigging for both masts should be. It is necessary to be careful when fitting one of the later lengths of standing rigging that you do not introduce too much tension so that earlier pieces become slack — all standing rigging should be taut.

The running rigging will, by its nature, be of smaller diameter but both this and the standing rigging will need small single or double blocks to run through (*Fig. 15*). Blocks on a ship are of various sizes, those on a barge being generally smaller than those on a barquentine. Ready-made blocks are available in a range of sizes but, having made my own wheels and deadeyes, I thought it would be interesting to try model blocks. 2.5mm styrene was used for a trial run and a slot was cut in the edge with the Minicraft table saw and then holes were drilled as shown in *Fig. 16*. The front edges were rounded and then the table saw used to form slots on both sides at right-angles to the edge, *Fig. 17* (the saw was adjusted to give a shallow cut by lowering the motor position). The saw was set for a deep cut to separate the strip and this was followed by the most delicate part — making the second longitudinal slot. Rounding of the final edges (*Fig. 18*) left one job — chopping the strip up into individual blocks. When it came to making smaller blocks for the barge I found that 1.5mm styrene was too fragile a material. What with holes drilled through and slots on four sides, the wretched things burst asunder when the wires were twisted around them (*Fig. 19*) so it was necessary to use the same technique as before but with brass, and it proved no more difficult than styrene, just somewhat longer.

To find thread suitable for the rigging was a matter of hunting round the shops. I bought a selection of thicknesses and shades, trying to avoid those which were hairy (cotton) in favour of man-made fibres, but some of the best were silk threads from a net and twine shop. I found that hairy threads could be de-haired by running them quickly through a flame but the conventional method is to plaster the hairs down with a liberal application of beeswax when the model is complete. I threaded them through blocks and deadeyes by using a very fine sewing needle and, for attaching blocks to masts or rigging, iron wire was used (*Fig. 19*) as copper wire is far too frail for the job. My model ships will never win gold medals at the Model Engineer Exhibition because, on the smaller spars, the threads were knotted in place instead of having yard bands to anchor them (*Fig. 10*) and even where such fittings were installed I knotted the threads to them instead of forming a lashing as in *Fig. 20*. On a real ship the ends of the running rigging are not left untidily lying around on the deck but are neatly coiled and hung up out of the way. One is unable to use gravity to form a neat rope arrangement — on the model the thread wants to unwind itself all

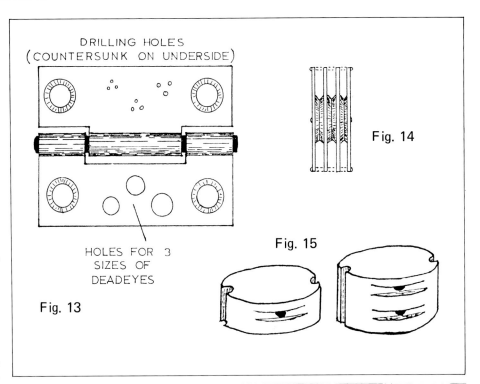

Three-masted topsail schooner Kathleen & May *and barquentine* Waterwitch.

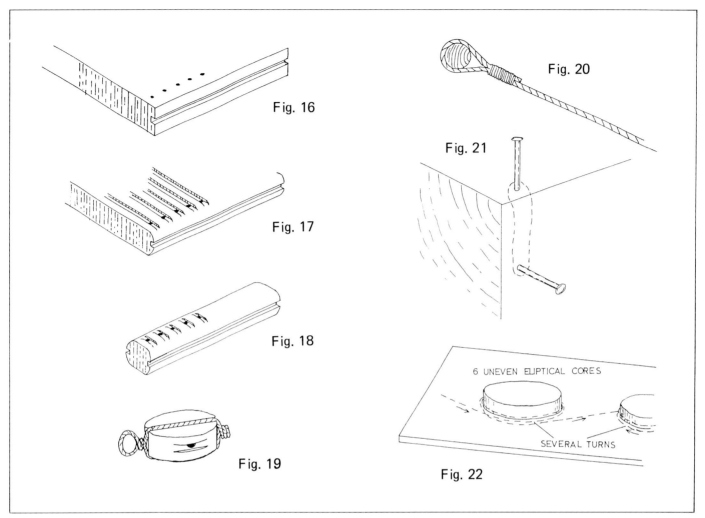

Fig. 16

Fig. 17

Fig. 18

Fig. 19

Fig. 20

Fig. 21

6 UNEVEN ELIPTICAL CORES

SEVERAL TURNS

Fig. 22

over the place, so I pre-formed them to the correct shape by making coils over nails (*Fig. 21*) and then soaking them in diluted wood glue. For large coils of heavier rope which are destined to lie on hatch covers, pieces of 3mm styrene on a 1mm styrene base acted as temporary cores while the glue-soaked thread dried out (*Fig. 22*). These coils, when dry, were very firm and could be fixed in place with a little Evo-stik. All knots in the rigging were given the diluted wood glue treatment before the ends were cut off close to the knot — this only takes a few minutes and can save the annoyance of re-rigging as a result of knots coming adrift.

Fig. 1d shows a ship's boat swung out over the side of the barge on its davits (swivelling supporting brackets from which it is hung) and the construction of this little boat was fairly easy. I carved a former to the correct shape from a piece of hardwood (*Fig. 23*) and coated it with silicone bath sealant to give a non-stick surface. The ½mm × ⅛mm styrene ribs were held in place with rubber bands and were given a steaming (*Fig. 24*). The keel was cemented in place and 0.25mm × 3mm microstrip planks were added. Next day, when all was dry, the ribs were trimmed to the correct length, the boat was lifted off the former and internal detail was added.

Neat stowing of ropes on Kathleen & May.

I had clear-cut ideas about the sails, knowing that a superb effect could be obtained by using painted tinfoil which would give a perfect representation of furled sails, as it would hold all the creases so realistically. Those who had tried making furled sails in this scale expressed their doubts and said that I would be better off using tissue paper. All brilliant pioneers meet Doubting Thomases so I set to work to prove them wrong, only to find that tinfoil was hopeless and that tissue paper (of the paper handkerchief variety) gave just the effect I was after. These handkerchiefs were of two-ply construction and for furled sails they were split down to a single layer while being kept double where set sails were required (tinfoil did however produce some excellent tarpaulins over the hatches of another vessel). The sails of a Thames barge should be the russet brown colour of the ochre and oil with which they are tanned and I now think that I sprayed mine with too red a hue, a matter which you could judge for yourself if only this cheapskate magazine would run to colour. On my model the main sail is pulled back against the mast (brailed), and ropes named on the plans are brails are used to draw the sail into this position. Real sails are not formed from one single sheet of material — they are assembled from two-foot wide bolts of canvas. Billings kits have material supplied with them for the sails and I have seen this fabric cut out, with sewing machine stitches to represent the seams between strips of canvas; the material is far too stiff and the stitching looks grotesque, so something far more delicate is essential. After the sprayed-on colour had dried I made a representation of the stitching lines with a soft pencil which did not tear the paper if used gently. The edges were turned over and glued down to make a hem. A vessel under way (sailing) will have varying amounts of sail set according to the wind conditions but few modellers will have reason to show a ship in this state — a more likely setting would be to have it berthed at a quay. When the ship is moored, the sails would not be set but would be in one of three other states: stowed away below deck leaving bare masts and spars if they were not going to be needed for some time; tightly furled (folded and bound to the masts and spars); hung loosely to dry out if the vessel arrived with the sails wet, necessary to prevent rotting if the sails were to be stored or furled for some time. For drying they were hung flapping loosely (like washing) so that they would not catch the wind. The first configuration is obviously the easy one and the second is not too time-consuming, while the third would look marvellous but my attempts at it were a dismal failure.

Painting the model was a straightforward job employing matt Precision Paints products. For all vessels, dirty-black was used for the hulls although the barge had a variation on this with the upper portion in light grey streaked with rust from its nails. The deck was made a 'dirty wood' colour and the coamings buff with red ochre hatch covers. The winches are green but the masts and spars are varnished wood, the

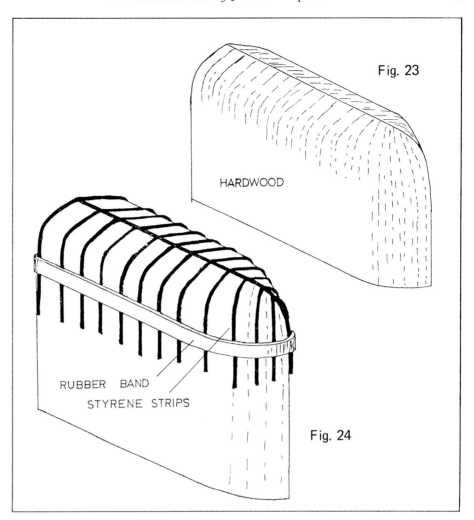

Fig. 23

HARDWOOD

RUBBER BAND

STYRENE STRIPS

Fig. 24

latter effect being obtained by using paint. All my masts and spars were painted SR Wagon Stone and when this was dry BR Bauxite was painted on very thinly with a stiff bristled brush which allowed some of the stone colour to show through and the streaky effect seemed to resemble the varnished masts which I had studied at St Katherine's Dock. I had used black silk for the barge rigging so this was painted grey to represent galvanised wire when all was in place.

The name of the barge is displayed on either side of the bow and across the stern. On a ship the letters are a minimum of six inches high and mine were produced by using white Letraset on black paper, then reduced by photocopying.

A rough guess would be about 250 hours' work for the barge model and I really enjoyed making it, as I did all the ships. It had been my original intention to make three of them, have a break for a few months working on some other part of the diorama, and then construct the other two, but such was the pleasure they gave me that I made all five consecutively. Would that I could make locos so readily! Before you pen an angry letter to the editor, I will admit to the discrepancies. What are *Kathleen & May* and *Waterwitch* doing in an 1840 dock scene? Sprit-sail barges were around in the 1790s but

— steel wire rope in 1840? Lack of accurate plans for an 1840s barge caused me to model *Venta* whose plans, I note, were drawn in 1971, which would indicate that the vessel may have been preserved and that somewhere around the coast of south-east England it is possibly available for photography.

Scottish Maid, the original 1:50 scale model with which I started, was to be sold when completed in order to recoup the cost of the kit, but Shirley didn't want to part with it so it is now in a glass showcase in our lounge (while its 4mm scale version is moored behind a warehouse — it didn't compare too favourably with its four successors!).

TOOLS & MATERIALS

The Minicraft saw mentioned in the text is a great asset and goodness knows how I ever managed without a Minicraft drill (both available from Nathan Shestopal, Unit 2, Sapcote Trading Centre, 374 High Road, Willesden, London NW10 2DH); apart from these two items nothing special is required.

Nothing very unusual was required except possibly some lead for anchors and a recommendation to avoid the copper-plated steel chain which is readily available and use the

vastly superior brass chain available from Mike Sharman, 10 Swindon Road, Cricklade, Swindon, Wilts.

Two good shops for ship modelling if you want timber kits, threads for rigging or ready made parts (blocks, deadeyes, ships' boats, etc) are Maritime Models, 7 Nelson Road, Greenwich, London SE10 and Euro Models, 35 Crown Road, Saint Margaret's, Twickenham, Middlesex. I am sure there are many other good suppliers but I have only seen the stocks of these two firms.

PLANS

Scale drawings of sailing ships, paddle steamers, merchant ships, fishing boats and barges are available from D. MacGregor Plans, 99 Lonsdale Road, London SW13 9DA (catalogue £1.50, including postage).

A catalogue of working drawings for 70 scale sailing ship models by H. A. Underhill is available at £1.30 while a catalogue of 35 working drawings for power vessels, also by Underhill cost £1.00, both from Bassett-Lowke Ltd., Harvey Reeves Road, Northampton NN5 5JR (postage extra). Both the MacGregor plans and the Bassett-Lowke range of plans are stocked at Maritime Models of Greenwich who also hold a large stock of books on ships and ship modelling. Albion Scott Ltd, 51 York Road, Brentford, Middlesex also hold a good selection of books.

FURTHER READING

If you ever want to model a Thames spritsail barge then you must have *Modelling Thames Sailing Barges* by E. C. Freeston and B. Kent from Conway Maritime Press, 7 Nelson Road, Greenwich, London SE10. This book has photographs of both actual barges and superb models along with many detail sketches. Throughout the text all measurements of the actual vessel are given, making it easy to model any scale.

Other helpful books are:

Spritsail Barges of the Thames and Medway (230pp) by E. J. March (David and Charles)

The Sailing Barges of Maritime England (80pp) by T. Ellis (Shepperton-Swan)

Sailing Barges (32pp) by M. Hazell (Shire Album)

Kathleen (The history of a spritsail sailing barge including an account of its restoration) by R. Walsh (Terence Dalton)

A Cross in the Topsail (a most interesting book about the large coasting barges owned by R. & W. Paul Ltd. of Ipswich) by R. Finch (Boydell)

Westcountry Coasting Ketches (70 photographs of ketches with extensive notes on each plus drawings of four vessels. Unfortunately for the modeller, these do not include the lines of the hulls) by W. J. Slade and B. Greenhill (Conway Maritime Press)

Ships and Ship Models by D. MacGregor (Argus)

The Techniques of Ship Modelling by G. A. Wingrove (Argus)

Building and Detailing Model Sailing Ships by G. E. Campbell (Argus)

Period Ship Modelling by R. K. Battson (Argus)

Making Model Ships Fittings (Argus)

A Ship Modeller's Manual by J. Bowen (Conway Maritime Press)

Ship Building in Miniature (this should be called 'Ship Building in sub-Miniature' as the models are full detailed at a scale of ⅓mm = 1 foot. Little use for the railway modeller but absolutely fascinating reading) (136pp) by D. McNarry (Conway Maritime Press)

All the Bassett-Lowke sailing ship plans are by H. A. Underhill who also wrote *Plank on Frame Models, Scale Masting and Rigging, Sailing Ship Rigs and Rigging* and *Masting and Rigging the Clipper Ship and Ocean Carrier*. I gather that these four books constitute the bible of ship modelling.

Plans can be enlarged or reduced to different scales by using an office photocopier with zoom facility but as A3 paper is the largest size which such machines normally handle one has to paste up separate pieces of the copied drawing. It is possible to use the reprographic services offered by specialist firms and have plans enlarged or reduced onto paper or film. One of the companies offering this facility is Variscale, 9 Park Place, Clifton, Bristol BS8 1JP.

GNR No. 63

It all began when a friend gave me a pair of 'plain' 7ft driving wheels. They had come off a Midland 'Spinner' 4–2–2 which he had built some years ago when one had a much smaller choice of wheels than today. As well as being a bit small, they were actually standard 22-spoked wheels from which the crank bosses had been laboriously turned and filed away. They looked quite good but my friend had decided to replace them with a correct pair of AGH ones. "You can chuck 'em away if you can't find a use for them" he said. My many boxes of spares testify to the fact that I am not good at throwing things away, so I began to look for photos of a suitable Single.

I had always fancied having a go at this type of engine but nothing of the kind would actually be right on my LNER (ex-GER) Wingham Branch, with its 1930s time-fix. This was duly pointed out by well-meaning friends but, being less of a purist than some people seem to think, I was prepared to stretch a point by a mere 30 or 40 years if only for the challenges involved. One or two friends have built beautiful models of James Holden's GER 2–2–2 and 4–2–2 classes but these have never been engines I have particularly wanted to build for myself. I rather like the 'Johnsonised' Midland Kirtley 2–2–2 engines (which, like all the above, have 7ft drivers), but when I saw those curvaceous outside frames and footplate platform, not to mention no less than 12 external springs (possibly unobtainable as castings), I closed the Midland book. What I wanted was a nice simple little engine as an interlude to more serious modelling – a quickie, in fact. Then I spotted Patrick Stirling's GNR 'No. 6' Class 2–2–2 engines – 7ft drivers, no external springs at all, a plain, no nonsense 'straightback' without even a dome to turn! Introduced in 1868, they just predated the 'eight-footers' and the last two emerged from Doncaster after the famous No. 1. Ivatt rebuilt four of them around the turn of the century with larger, domed boilers pitched higher to clear the driving wheels, giving them an ugly Humpty-Dumpty look; fortunately, the remaining eight retained their Victorian elegance, lasting into the early years of the 20th century. Many ended their days on the level Fenland lines between Peterborough and Boston – next door, in fact, to my chosen GER and M&GN lines at Spalding. One of these would do nicely; the slotted splashers might prove a bit tricky but otherwise, no problems – so I thought!

A pair of cast-off driving wheels launched DERYCK FEATHERSTONE on a 7mm model of one of Stirling's elegant Great Northern Railway Singles. But first, he had to delve into the strange and intricate geometry devised by Victorian draughtsmen to decorate the engines. It seems they weren't quite so plain and simple as they looked . . .

RESEARCH AND DRAWINGS
In a chapter on the eight-footers, the late F.C. Hambledon, in his priceless book *Locomotives Worth Modelling*, has a side elevation of one of these engines at a scale of about 4.5mm–1ft. From this I did some trial 7mm scale drawings to test for motor clearances etc; then a friend lent me a beautiful 1½in–1ft copy of the original Doncaster drawing and I was finally hooked. Luckily, there are quite a lot of good photos in various sources and there is a chapter on the class in the RCTS *Great Northern Locomotive History Pt. 2*. As a prototype, I finally settled on No. 63, of which there is a splendid full-page photo from circa 1892/3 in *G.N.R. Engine Sheds Vol 1*. A local engineer with a large photocopier ran me a couple of copies of the GA drawing and I returned the original, it being my rule never to take valuable original drawings into the workshop.

There was no similar drawing of the tender and, in any case, the class seemed to have run with many different tenders over the years. The photo showed that, in her later years, No. 63 had a Stirling type 'F'. These varied in height according to water capacity and the one in the photo seemed to be of medium size and the top of the tank (below the flaring) was almost exactly in line with the boiler handrail – i.e. about 3ft 9ins above the footplate. The one fitted to the preserved No. 1 is of the smaller, earlier kind and is bereft of the three attractive coal rails round the top. It is this tender which is drawn, again by F.C. Hambledon, in *HMRS Journal* Vol. 6 (1968/9), which I used to build up a drawing of the one I wanted. The GA drawing showed the original and revised cab sides but was too early, of course, to show the 2in

larger diameter boilers on a 1in higher centre-line, fitted to the class in the 'eighties. I had to make allowance for this and the consequently shorter chimney, as well as the later safety-valve 'trumpet' housing Ramsbottom valves instead of the original Salter types. Hambledon to the rescue again, bless him – he has dimensioned drawings of both types in his book.

Thus equipped, and, I thought, fully informed, I could hardly wait to make a start. I would point out that these preliminaries have been covered in detail for the benefit of readers who may be contemplating a model of any truly historic and less familiar prototype. Research and the thinking time involved can be as fascinating as the actual modelling, and I lived and breathed this little engine for weeks before I even cut out the frames.

I do not propose to give a blow-by-blow account of how I built No. 63 since most of the work was the sort of scratchbuilding practice which has been described in these pages many times. Instead I have selected a few of the more unusual features and attempted to show how I tackled the problems involved.

THE UNDERFRAME
For the motor I chose a Sagami 1833. This is a fairly slow-running unit and with 26:1 gears has proved amply powerful and not over-fast even with 7ft drivers. In order to clear the backhead, I scrapped the etched gearbox sides and built new ones to bring the motor as far forward as possible; even then I had to shorten the rear end of the motor shaft by about 5mm. These armature shafts are hardened and ordinary files and saws won't touch them, but you can get special triangular files for sharpening woodsaws

(which, of course, have hardened teeth), and with one of these I filed right round the shaft, holding the motor in my left hand with the shaft in a vice. A sharp twist with the shaft held between two pairs of pliers snapped the end off easily and cleanly – and I still had room for a small flywheel.

The rear and driving axles are unsprung, with a little down-play on the rear one. The front axle has plenty of up and down movement (about 1.5mm each way) and is sprung just enough to keep it on the rails without taking too much of the vital adhesive weight from the driving axle. Being on unfamiliar ground with my first Single, I gave a lot of thought to the question of weight; after all, there's not a lot of room and only one powered axle. It seemed that an obvious place for ballast was the firebox/ashpan unit, so I made this as a brass box with embossed visible rivets and then added a few real ⅓₂in ones in strategic places to hold it together during the next process. The assembly was embedded in a margarine box of damp soil and filled with molten lead. This sort of foundry work is great fun but I always do it out of doors, using a cat-food tin with a spout nipped in it and fitted with a stout wire handle. Scrap bits of whitemetal kits and odd lumps of lead are melted down over a gas blowlamp. For safety I wear leather gardening gloves and protective glasses and hold the handle with a pair of heavy duty pliers, standing well clear when pouring – molten lead is too hot to take chances with, so don't! Other weights were later cast for the boiler and sandboxes using moulds from scrap wood.

The brake gear could best be described as 'interesting', especially the linkage to the trailing wheels. Outside brake rodding is a fruitful source of shorts so I always apply liberally Araldited tissue paper to the inner faces of the rods; when fully cured and cleaned up, it cannot be seen. I have treated several engines like this and have never had any trouble.

At the last moment I decided to fit dummy motion between the frames as there seemed to be a lot of empty space in front of the sandboxes. So much for this being a 'quickie'!

LOCO BODY

When this article was first offered to MRJ, the editor suggested that I comment on the importance of keeping the lines and angles of such a 'plain' engine really straight and true. I agree that multi-level, curved footplates and lots of fittings and plumbing can sometimes disguise minor deviations from the straight and narrow but all I can add applies to any scratchbuilt model, ancient or modern, and even to kit-built ones: in a nutshell (A) Don't hesitate to consign any inaccurate or doubtful piece to the scrap box and (B) Don't waste time trying to botch up errors during assembly; instead, unsolder – if necessary right down to component parts – and start again. This kind of quality control is usually quicker in the long run. It is a skilled (or

Right driving wheel. Note brake linkage.

Rear left underframe. Note wire pick-ups on insulated PCB plate which also carries the sandpipe.

lucky) modeller indeed who is never faced with these decisions.

I thought long and hard about the slotted splashers. In the 'eighties the slots had been blanked-off with a sheet of metal behind. There were therefore three layers, if you count the 2in broad brass band visually separating the splasher itself from the sandboxes. There seemed to be three ways of doing it; commission a manufacturer to photo-etch the slots and beading, make a template and get a friend in the trade to profile mill the slots, or have a go at it myself by hand. Both the first two options would involve expense and delay and, besides, I really wanted to do it myself. In any case an accurate drawing was required and this was the big problem. I had made both 7mm and large-scale drawings from Hambledon's diagram but they didn't look quite right. Finally, poring over the Doncaster drawing for the fiftieth time, I found the

answer. With the drawing stretched out on a table, I located the tiny marks made by the draughtsman's compasses 125 years ago to draw the top and bottom semi-circles of the slots. With a fine Rotring pen, I extended lines through these points to cross what should have been the axle vertical centreline. To my surprise, the lower slots were angled from a point 1½in *above* the axle centreline, the next ones from 5in *below* and the upper ones 8in below. Having no common centre, there was, of course no regular angle between the slots, although the outer end circles were spaced 1ft 11in apart (see *Fig. 1*). Complicated? I'll say it was! It's true that in 7mm scale these measurements are quite small, but my next drawing began to look right and I was immediately struck by the resemblance to the paddleboxes of some of the old-time steamers. Such were the aesthetics of 19th century locomotive design.

A dummy run on a piece of nickel-silver large enough to include these assorted centres didn't seem too difficult, so I sweated two pieces together and marked out the splasher/sandboxes, slots and all. The critical thing was to get the end circles dead right so I used a strong light and magnifier and started with smaller drills, enlarging in stages to the final diameter. All I then had to do was to cut along the straights and clean up. After all the hours of drawing, the job was quickly done. The beading was made by turning a ring from brass, a circle being enough for the two sides. It was parted off about 0.5mm thick and filed down after soldering on.

The only other unusual job was making the two buffer beams. In the prototype they were of sandwich construction, consisting of a 5in plank of oak between two ½in plates of iron. I used a piece of beech 3mm thick between two pieces of 0.25mm NS. The plates were soldered together, drilled for buffers and couplings, and filed to size. After separating, the outer ones were embossed for rivets. The wood beams were left oversize but also drilled for buffers so that the three parts could be lined up with temporary bolts. They were stuck with Araldite and cleaned up when cured. I was smugly pleased with the result until I tried to solder the front one to the footplate platform, when it promptly sprang apart! The expansion of the thin metal against the inert wood was the obvious cause (next time I'll think first!); the problem was solved by scratching the metal to provide a key for the adhesive and then fitting the coupling hook, side chain shackles and buffer stocks before soldering. The tender guard irons were also attached with rivets right through the beams.

The rest of the engine and tender bodywork was fairly straightforward but I did have a few problems with the fittings either through lack of information or unfamiliarity with the subject, and the following may be of interest.

The Vacuum Ejector

Following the adoption by the Great Northern of the dangerously unsatisfactory non-automatic vacuum brake in 1875, these and other engines were fitted with large live steam ejectors on the right-hand side of the smokebox. This was retained and adapted to the automatic brake after 1885. Of course the GA drawing did not show this fitting, which came some 17 years after the drawing was made. Hambledon's drawing was a bit vague in this area but by using it and scaling up several broadside photos, I arrived at a fairly convincing drawing of the apparatus (*Fig. 2*). The main body was turned from brass rod and the rest from brass wire with turned collars to represent flanges.

Cab Fittings

These old Stirling cabs certainly reveal all, although the controls were rudimentary compared with more modern engines. The GA showed clearly the firebox door, one sandbox

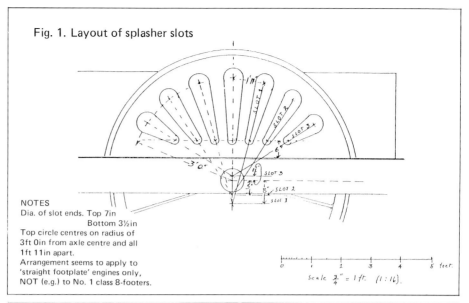

Fig. 1. Layout of splasher slots

NOTES
Dia. of slot ends. Top 7in
Bottom 3½in
Top circle centres on radius of
3ft 0in from axle centre and all
1ft 11in apart.
Arrangement seems to apply to
'straight footplate' engines only,
NOT (e.g.) to No. 1 class 8-footers.

Test piece.

Slotted splasher. Boiler feed pipe not yet lined up!

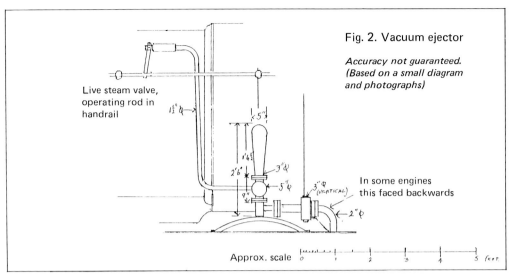

Fig. 2. Vacuum ejector

*Accuracy not guaranteed.
(Based on a small diagram
and photographs)*

Live steam valve,
operating rod in
handrail

In some engines
this faced backwards

Approx. scale

*The vacuum ejector. Note the 'onion'
cylinder lubricator had to be moved
forward.*

lever, the huge reverse lever and the typical GN
double-ended pull-out regulator. Hambledon's
'No.1' cab drawing added a water gauge, one
steam pressure dial, a blower handle and little
else. These, I assumed would be standard fittings
but after 1885 there must also have been a driver's vacuum brake valve, plus a vacuum gauge
somewhere up near the steam one. To have
added any more would have been guesswork
and, in any case, I felt that a couple of cast figures would conceal most of the errors and
omissions.

Smokebox Door
This was very much a 'how' rather than a 'what'
problem. Most 19th-century engines had thin
smokebox doors, slightly dished in the middle,
which fitted flush into a recess in the smokebox
front plate. In many old photos, the door rim
can only be seen as a faint circular line. Most
engines surviving into this century had these
doors replaced by heavy cast ones with
machined rims which gave a better seal and a
longer life. However, No. 63 and her unrebuilt
sisters carried the old flat type to the end.

I cut out and filed up together three smokebox end plates. Two were soldered to the wrapper to make the box in the normal way. The
other one had its edge rounded so that when
added to the front it gave a good impression of
the prototype flanged plate (*Fig. 3*). Before fitting, I mounted this plate on a hardwood block
on the lathe faceplate, located dead centre by
means of a screw, and parted off the centre,
leaving a hole the size of the door. This would
be a tedious job with a piercing saw and files
but not too difficult for the latheless modeller.
The door was turned from brass and finished
with a thickness of 0.5mm at the rim, the same
as the front plate.

Chimney
After producing an acceptable rendering of the
tricky safety-valve trumpet, the apparently simple one-piece Ivatt chimney, as carried by this
engine in the photo, went wrong at the top and
I had to start again (perhaps I was deceived by

Fig. 3. Smokebox front (not to scale)

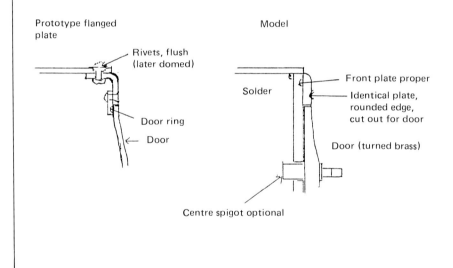

Prototype flanged
plate

Rivets, flush
(later domed)

Door ring

Door

Model

Solder

Front plate proper

Identical plate,
rounded edge,
cut out for door

Door (turned brass)

Centre spigot optional

Chimney lamp iron.

its simplicity). The second one was OK but
there remained the problem of the lamp iron
half way up; just to solder it on flat would
almost guarantee its loss the first time anyone
tried to put a lamp on it. I fold my lamp irons
from strips of tinplate, filling the folds with solder, and cut each iron off from the strip as
required. A 'tail' is left which can be pushed
through the supporting surface and soldered.
Wingham Branch operators insist on correct
headlamp codes (usually) and these irons have
proved very durable. However, it was not easy
to make the necessary slot in the thick brass of
the chimney even though it was bored out as
much as possible. I managed to bore two
0.6mm holes without breaking the drill and
then made a tiny flat broach from an old needle
file and broke through between the holes by
tapping and wiggling. After coating with solder
paste, the tail was pushed through and the

whole thing was heated with a pencil torch till the solder ran (*Fig. 4*).

The whole business of the placing of lamp irons on these old GN engines worried me. Why two on each side of the platform and none in the middle? Why one on the smokebox top and this extra one up the chimney? Eventually a friend in the Great Northern Society came up with the answer: the chimney iron was used, in the old GN code, to carry a lamp *extra* to the normal descriptive code if the train was a special working for which no written notice had been given to signalmen. After 1902 the RCH standard code was adopted by the GN and the chimney irons became redundant. They were fairly soon removed from most classes, but I suppose the life expectancy of the remaining unrebuilt 2–2–2s was limited, so nobody bothered and they carried this historic fitting to the end. The extra ones over the buffers seem to have been used to carry spare lamps, facing backwards, and, as the RCH code required a central position, one of these seems to have been moved to the centre. Study of photographs reveals that the other 'twin' remained in place, sometimes into LNER and even BR days! (information courtesy of Trevor Mullins).

No.63 ON THE ROAD

In a bare metal state, the engine was thoroughly tested and run-in on the Wingham Branch, which includes on its outdoor main line a formidable ⅜th scale mile of 1-in-72. Held at signals at the top of this, she restarted a train of five six-wheelers and also performed well with five heavy Gresley bogies. On level track in the yard, trains of almost twice this weight have been shunted. Performance is well up to the best I had hoped. The total weight is 985gms, about 2lbs 3oz, of which I reckon about half is

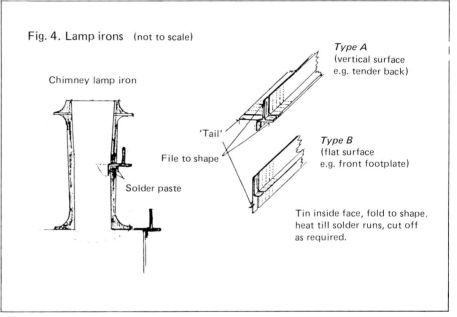

Fig. 4. Lamp irons (not to scale)

Chimney lamp iron

'Tail'

File to shape

Solder paste

Type A
(vertical surface
e.g. tender back)

Type B
(flat surface
e.g. front footplate)

Tin inside face, fold to shape, heat till solder runs, cut off as required.

Buffer and 'sandwich' beam.

available for adhesion as the engine is almost balanced, fore-and-aft, on the driving axle, but with a slight bias towards the back. An early experiment with a weighted tender pressing onto a fixed drawbar proved useless as it merely loaded the trailing axle and actually reduced adhesion.

During these trials, my version of Mr Stirling's pretty little seven-footer aroused mixed feelings and produced remarks and such mocking cries as: "Deryck, the coupling rods have dropped off!" I felt it was all worthwhile if only to have stirred my friends up a bit! Things may be a bit different now that No.63 has returned from Alan Brackenborough resplendent in the full glory of the old Great Northern passenger livery.

PETTIGREW'S FURNESS PASSENGER ENGINES OF 1901

Drawn and described by MIKE PEASCOD:

William Pettigrew was appointed Locomotive Superintendent of the Furness Railway in 1897, moving from the post of Works Manager at Nine Elms Works on the London & South Western Railway. In the first few years of his tenure he faced acute problems in the form of lack of capacity in the goods engines used by the railway. His very first design for the Furness Railway was a class of six-coupled goods engines which came into service in 1899, and whilst they did not entirely put matters right, they at least went a long way to improve the situation, so he was able to turn his attention to improving the passenger fleet, again in some trouble through a lack of capacity.

The four-coupled design had, by then, been established as the norm for express passenger work on the Furness Railway. The first of the type were acquired in 1890 when four intended for use on the Cambrian Railways were purchased, and a further six of an enlarged version were built in 1896. These ten engines were to standard Sharp, Stewart designs and went some way in improving the passenger capacity, but by 1899 they were the only engines available for the increasing passenger duties and there was a distinct feeling that if something wasn't done soon they would be worked into the ground. It was intended that a further six engines of even larger size should be ordered, to be available for the summer traffic of 1900, but the time required for detailing work on the new design was too short. To be sure of having something available for the summer peak traffic period, a further pair similar to the 1896 engines were built to fill the gap, the designs and patterns being readily available and allowing a quick turnround of the order. These engines did, however, take advantage of some of the ideas that had been planned for the new engines, particularly the larger, 3,000 gallon tenders in place of the original 2,500 gallon types.

Pettigrew's earlier designs for the Furness Railway were influenced by some of the Adams LSWR engines. The Class X2 engines of 1890–92, whilst somewhat larger, were clearly the basis for Pettigrew's 1901 design. Similarities can

This view of No. 126 in Furness days gives a good overall impression of these stylish engines.
K. NORMAN

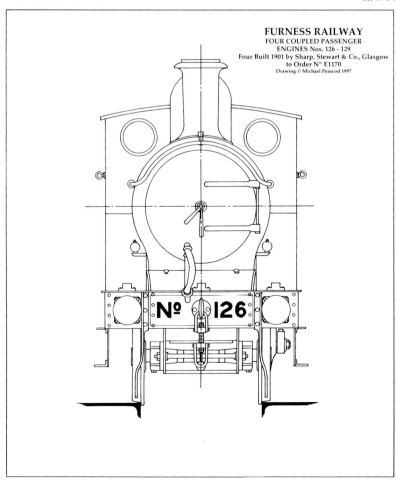

FURNESS RAILWAY
FOUR COUPLED PASSENGER
ENGINES Nos. 126 - 129
Four Built 1901 by Sharp, Stewart & Co., Glasgow
to Order Nº E1170
Drawing © Michael Peascod 1997

Nº 126

also be found in his first six-coupled tender and tank engines. The most striking difference between the two four-coupled designs was that the X2 had outside cylinders, a feature that could not be considered on the Furness due to a more restrictive loading gauge. The reduced order of four engines were built by Sharp, Stewart and delivered in time for the 1901 season and numbered 126 to 129 in the Furness list. They were considered as 'new' to the locomotive stock, the cost being charged to the capital account. Details of the new engines are as follows:

FR No.	LMS No.	Prog No.	Withdrawn
126	10143	4716	Dec 1931
127	10144	4717	May 1930
128	10145	4718	Jun 1930
129	10146	4719	Jan 1931

They were used primarily on the Carnforth–Whitehaven through trains — Nos. 126 and 128 were based at the south end of the line at Carnforth and the other pair were shedded at the other end of the line at Corkickle. They remained at the top of the passenger link until the introduction of more modern four-coupled engines in 1913–1914. Later in their service, the operation of trains north of the natural Furness Railway boundary at Whitehaven began when a number of passenger trains were worked through to Carlisle. This change in operation is thought to have been introduced as an expedient during the First World War. They used the No. 2 bay at Citadel Station, sharing it with the more normal Maryport & Carlisle Railway trains.

At grouping, they were renumbered 10143 to 10146 in the LMS list and continued with their normal duties until withdrawal. Nos. 10144 and 10146 were withdrawn in 1930, and Nos. 10143 and 10146 went to the scrap line the following year.

LIVERY

The later style of Furness Railway livery was used on these engines. The customary Indian red was bordered with a 2in square-cornered band edged with a ¼in vermilion line. The inner lining was 1½in wide, edged inside and out with a vermilion line. This inner band had rounded corners and was separated from the edging by some 1½in of the base colour. The positioning of the lining is shown on the main drawing, though no attempt has been made to represent the vermilion lines — the small sketch of the corner detail will

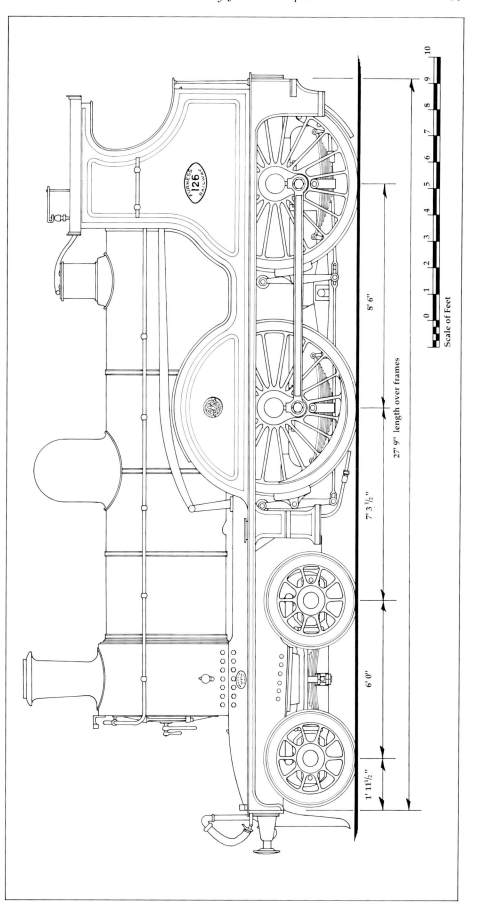

FURNESS RAILWAY

**3,000 GALLON TENDER FOR FOUR COUPLED
PASSENGER ENGINES Nos. 126 - 129
Four Built 1901 by Sharp, Stewart & Co., Glasgow
to Order Nº T1170**

Drawing © Michael Peascod 1997

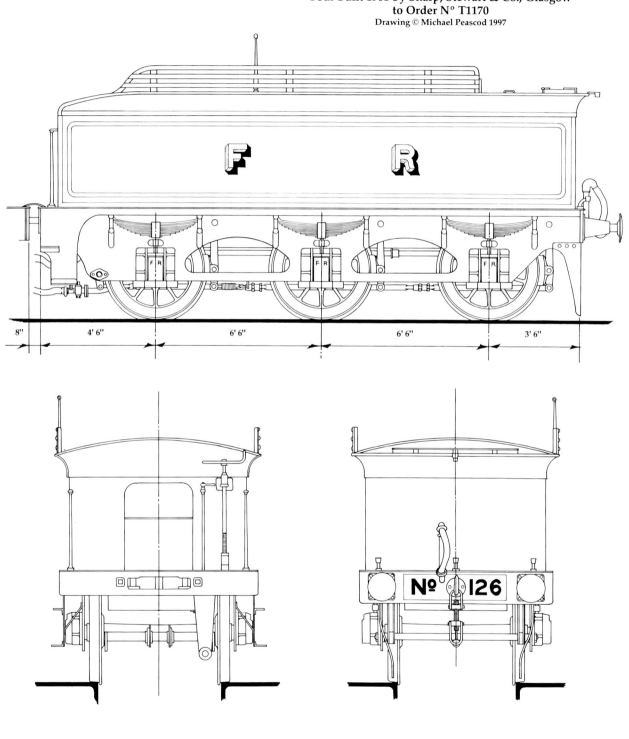

8"   4' 6"   6' 6"   6' 6"   3' 6"

Nº 126

0 1 2 3 4 5 6 7 8 9 10

Scale of Feet

give an idea of the disposition of the colours. The front splasher of the engine carried the 'locomotive' crest showing predominantly red colouring. This crest differed from the 'carriage' crest in that the latter was predominantly blue. The number plate consisted of brass figures on a black ground, the figures being without serifs. The maker's plate, on the front frames, was polished brass with raised letters with SHARP, STEWART in the top arc, GLASGOW in the lower and the maker's number in a straight line across the centre of the plate.

The front buffer beam was painted black with a central vermilion panel, a white line separating the two colours. The locomotive number was shown in cut-out brass characters. Boiler bands were black edged with vermilion.

The tender was lined with a single panel with the letters F and R in gold, shaded blue and light blue to the left, with black counter shading to the right. The rear buffer beam was treated in the same manner as the engine, including again the engine number.

The LMS passenger livery of lined red was applied to all of the engines of the class, with large running numbers on the tenders.

At grouping, LMS livery was applied to the engines. No. 10144 (FR No. 127) is seen between turns at Bransty station, Whitehaven, probably after working a Carlisle to Whitehaven train. Note the LMS crest is applied to the cab side sheet.

REAL PHOTOGRAPHS

Four-Coupled Bogie Passenger Engines, 1901 — Table of Dimensions

Cylinders (2)	
Diameter	18in
Stroke	26in
Boiler	
Length	10ft 8⅜in
Diameter inside	4ft 3in
Height of centre of boiler from rails	7ft 5in
Tubes	
Number	230
Diameter outside	1¾in
Heating surfaces	
Tubes	1,154.75 sq ft
Firebox	108.5 sq ft
Total	1,263.25 sq ft
Grate area	17.75 sq ft
Working pressure	160lbs/sq in
Wheels	
Coupled wheels	6ft 6in
Bogie wheels	3ft 6in
Capacity	
Water	3,000 gallons
Coal	3 tons 10 cwt
Dimensions	
Length of engine frames	27ft 9in

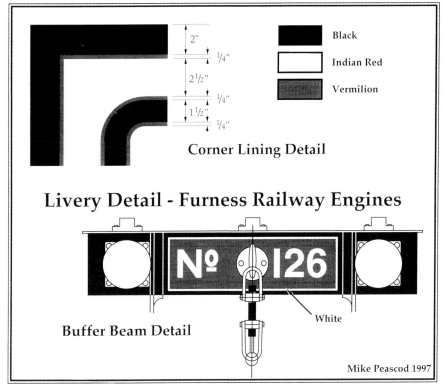

Livery Detail - Furness Railway Engines

Corner Lining Detail

Buffer Beam Detail

Black

Indian Red

Vermilion

White

Mike Peascod 1997

SHOCK TACTICS *continued from page 44*

balls. The use of two ball-bearings per runner was necessary at this stage to ensure that the plastic angles were parallel to the brass ones in both the horizontal and vertical planes. Pieces of Plastruct T were then slid down inside the body and glued to the tops of the plastic angles and the inside faces of the body sides. This correctly located the body on the chassis. The body with its runners was then removed from the chassis and the joints reinforced with bits of scrap plastic. End stops were also fitted to the V-grooves. A piece of Plastruct T was also cemented to the inside of one end of the body to receive the other end of the motion transfer link. It had to be drilled before installation, of course.

Two 6BA nuts were soldered to the top face of the floor, on the longitudinal centre line, one over each W-iron. Corresponding slots were cut in the transverse body members to take the retaining screws, which had to be just long enough to allow the body to move freely but not slack enough to allow the ball-bearings to fall out — the model won't work if it loses its marbles! When the body was assembled onto the chassis, only one ball-bearing per runner was used to give a true three-point mounting. The roof was made detachable for maintenance and was covered with a piece of manilla envelope, rough side out, to simulate the canvas covering of the prototype. The remaining detailing could then be done.

Alan Gibson axlebox-and-spring castings were used, with wheels from the same source. Brake shoes were cast in Milliput in a silicone rubber mould — a

piece of wire was moulded into the back which was soldered to the W-irons. When I came to paint the body I found my tin of enamel paint was going off, so I thinned it with Car Plan *cellulose* thinner, which worked a treat (I'm indebted to Brian Bassington of Chelmsford & District Model Railway Club for that tip). The rivet detail on the prototype appeared to be fairly low profile, possibly coach bolt

heads, so I cheated and applied them as dots of brown Rotring drawing ink with a mapping pen after spraying the body. Sprat & Winkle couplers were fitted, coupler at one end and wire loop at the other, since stock on my layout cannot get turned end-for-end in service — I usually fit the coupler to the rigid W-iron. Total construction time including painting and rectifications, 25 hours.

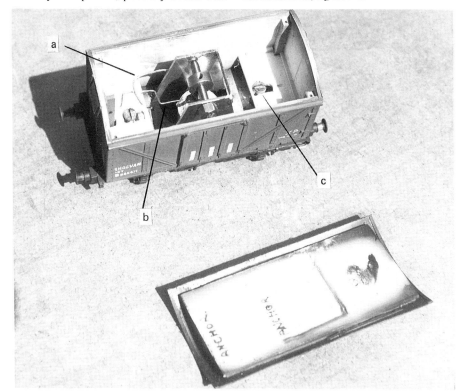

Piece of wire 'a' retains motion transfer link 'b' when vehicle is inverted for wheel cleaning. 'c' = body retaining screw. The inscription 'Anchor' on the underside of the roof is just to tell me which way round to put the roof on. Being a hand-made model, it fits better the way round it was originally made.

This GWR 'County' class 4 – 6 – 0 is a 4mm scale model built to P4 by Guy Williams especially for his new book More 4mm Engines.

THE ART DECO LEGEND

One of the more unusual aspects of finescale railway modelling is that we tend, by and large, to be fairly disciplined about our choice of subject. Although I could be wrong, I get the impression that our military, aviation and ship modelling confrères have a far more catholic approach. Within reason they can and do pick on pretty well anything that takes their fancy. Some might specialise in Japanese bombers or American AFVs while others go more for the diorama approach but, on the whole, they tend to be much less specific in their interests than we are.

Our urge to model each and everything that takes our fancy is, in theory at any rate, tempered by the requirements of our layouts. If we choose to model, say, the Cleator & Workington Railway in 1910 with any degree of accuracy, then we will try and stick, for authenticity's sake, to an appropriate, if restricted, selection of locomotives, rolling stock and other accoutrements. Though there are many drawbacks to the tyranny of the layout-oriented approach — as opposed to the construction of one-off models, without any overall scheme — it does constitute an approach to modelling that is far more integrated and systematic than any other that I know of. At the very least it gives a purpose to our work and stops us disappearing down too many blind alleys.

Such monogamy can, however, lead to a certain monotony and I find it is refreshing, once in a while, to have a little dabble in someone else's backyard. I think a lot

Many people were aware that a vast and unique experimental locomotive was roaming the rails, but few had actually seen it. Thus, Gresley's bizarre 4-6-4 — a great Art Deco sausage of a machine — became known as 'Hush-Hush'. When South Eastern Finecast produced a 4mm kit, TIM SHACKLETON couldn't resist it:

of modellers feel the same way, and for the same reason. Like many others I have, over the years, built a small and scatty collection of models that interest me but can have no possible relevance to any railway I am ever likely to build — an Ivatt 'Duchess', an LNER dynamometer car and a Bulleid diesel among several others. I model them purely because they appeal to me.

When I first became interested in railways there were three engines that, more than any others, I particularly wanted to see. One was the very last Garratt, No. 47994, and another was the loco that spotters dubbed the 'Un-named Streak', the solitary Class W1 4-6-4 No. 60700. The third was the 'Leader' but that, I soon learned, was long gone. I liked these engines because they were different and unique but unfortunately all of them were scrapped before they could become a thin black line in my Ian Allan ABC. Thirty-odd years went by before it struck me that I could always do the next best thing and model them. By this time I realised that No. 60700 hadn't always looked like a stretched-out A4 but had begun life late in 1929 as something even more out of the ordinary, a hefty 'Hudson' chassis on which Gresley had mounted an experimental marine-type boiler with a working

pressure of 450psi. Built to the extreme limits of the loading gauge, this stupendous kettle was shrouded in a bulbous casing from which massive elephant-ear smoke deflectors protruded, emphasising rather than hiding the fact that the engine appeared to possess neither smokebox nor chimney.

I've always loved the look of this engine which, visually as well as technically, was a real one-off. It had something of the ring of Art Deco and I can't think of anything quite like it anywhere else in the world, although it seems to anticipate some of the great American streamlined locomotives of the 1930s — the New York Central Hudsons, for instance. The great industrial designer Raymond Loewy was, of course, involved with styling a number of American locomotives and I am sure that the extraordinary outline of Gresley's W1 was not entirely the product of a railway drawing office — it looks more like an outstanding piece of product design than a railway engine. Most purely experimental locomotives have been spectacularly ugly — think of the Ljungstrom turbine, for instance, or the Fell diesel — but here one senses elements of indulgence, as if someone very important had decided that the engine was going to break new ground aesthetically as well as thermodynamically. The Hush-Hush, it should be pointed out, preceded by some years the appearance of other streamlined express locomotives in Britain, the infinitely better known Gresley A4s, Stanier 'Coronations' and Bulleid Pacifics.

Despite having had several runs at H M le Fleming's exhaustive — and, for me, exhausting — technical profile of the W1 in the November 1955 *Trains Illustrated*, I still don't quite understand what was so special about Mr Harold Yarrow's water-tube boiler. The appearance of the locomotive has always been more than enough for me. Evidently it excited the contemporary imagination as well, for the W1 was a rare bird, cloaked in mystery, more of a rumour than a fact. It was seldom photographed and it became known as the Hush-Hush locomotive. It was an eccentric aristocrat among engines and, aptly enough, it didn't appear to do an awful lot of work. In fact, despite a number of appearances on the 'Flying Scotsman' and other prestige expresses, the Hush-Hush turned out to be something of a delinquent. The loco existed in its original form for less than six years — much of its time being spent sidelined at Darlington Works — before it was reluctantly rebuilt

by Gresley as a conventional, firetube-boilered locomotive along the lines of his A4 Pacifics.

The Hush-Hush was based for most of its life at Gateshead but in its final year it moved to Neville Hill. Since it spent most of its restricted working life on East Coast main line expresses north of Newcastle and, later, on Newcastle–Leeds turns, it would be of extremely limited appeal to most modellers — although the engine was an exhibition regular at places as scattered as Leicester, Ipswich, Sheffield and Hull (prototype for everything department?). It has not, for obvious reasons, generated the groundswell of popular opinion that one hopes will, one day, lead to decent kits for locomotives as varied as a T9 or a B12.

Somewhere in the dim and distant I recall seeing a Gauge 1 model of the Hush-Hush but it was a considerable surprise to me when, in 1994, South Eastern Finecast introduced a kit for it. Not surprisingly, being bored with rakes of Dogfish or LMS suburban stock or whatever it was I was dutifully building at the time, I succumbed fairly quickly. There's a lot to be said, sometimes, for doing what you want rather than what you think you ought to be doing. The kit is typical of the

revamped Finecast range. The body and tender are whitemetal, the chassis and valve gear are in etched nickel silver, the instructions are well thought out and have particularly good exploded diagrams. Opening up the tissue wrappings, though, my first thoughts were that the pattern-making was not as impressive as on some of Finecast's other recent products — for my money the J39 and K3, revamped and remastered by the gifted Alistair Rolfe, are the best predominantly whitemetal kits I have come across.

It was obvious from the start that quite a bit of refinement would be called for if I was to create an effective model of a favourite locomotive. Some components of the Hush-Hush are common to other kits in the Finecast range, with consequent compromise in strict prototype accuracy. However, given the extremely limited commercial appeal of such a prototype, I can understand why certain economies might have been necessary and I am grateful that Finecast managed to get a kit on the market at all.

The Hush-Hush comes with a generic chassis and valve-gear fret which Finecast use for their other Gresley express locomotives and hence is not entirely correct for the W1. It is, however, reasonably *au*

courant and so, having sawn out the openings for the hornblocks, I made up the chassis more or less as supplied but ditched the screw-in tubular spacers, which I find have a propensity to induce minor twists and distortions, and substituted my own L-shaped spacers. My main modification to the chassis concerned the area around the driving wheels because this, in many designs, is often weakened due to the impossibility of fitting conventional spacers in among the pivots, motor mounts and so forth. Paradoxically this is the area in both prototype and model where the kinking and bowing that may result from inadequate bracing can least be tolerated. It should be noted that at the outer ends of the chassis — where there is usually more than enough room for generous cross-members — exact parallelism is far less critical.

My preferred solution to the problem is to solder lengths of 1/16 in brass capillary tube transversely across the chassis at the points from which the upper brake hangers will later be suspended. Wire can be passed through these from which the actual brake assembly is hung; the brass tubes have the extremely useful function of considerably stiffening the chassis at its most vulnerable points. I am aware that a pro-

The reassuring familiar bulk of the Gresley 8-wheel tender emphasises the extraordinary profile of the W1 in its original form. It would have looked absolutely stunning with a massive bogie tender such as those fitted to many American engines – but there was no need.

totype chassis will flex in motion but I have never found this to be a feature that scales down happily in model form. Because of the close spacing of the wheels — exacerbated when, as here, one is using Romfords — the brass tubes will need to be cut off flush with the outside of the frames to avoid electrical contact. I have made several sets of frames in this manner using nothing thicker than 20-thou brass and their rigidity is in the Dreadnought class, in marked contrast to the frailty of many etched chassis designs where it is usually all too easy to induce distortions during the ebb and flow of battle. The idea of the tubular cross-member/brake hanger is certainly not my own.

Once the frames had been assembled on a simple wooden jig, I installed the compensation. After experimenting with most of the available makes of hornblocks, I have settled, for some years past, on the MJT 'basic' design. I like the generous bearing surfaces against which the axleboxes slide, while the accurate fit of the components renders filing unnecessary. Rather unusually, assembly with epoxy resin is strongly recommended for these hornblocks and this is wise, since I have found through bitter experience that it is the devil's own job to get stray solder out of any of the bearing surfaces. As luck had it, I found that I had run out of the quick-setting Bostik epoxy and I didn't want to hang around for a whole day waiting for 24hr Araldite to go off. Feeling playful, I decided to see if I could make a better fist out of soldering them than the last time. A very light touch with a hot, clean iron is called for — resistance soldering comes into its own for this kind of work — and you need to be very confident of your soldering skills, otherwise stick (literally) with the epoxy.

Once assembled, I like to dunk the whole bearing in Brasso and rub each axlebox gently up and down in its slots until it runs smoothly but without any slop. This operation simulates about six months' wear in a couple of minutes. The final stage is to put short lengths of wire through the holes in the hornguides and bend them over to secure the bearings in place. There is no point wasting straight brass wire on this job and I employ instead those otherwise useless coils of wire which the less clued-up kit manufacturers insist on supplying in lieu of handrail wire — I have bales of the stuff

in my spares boxes. I then mount the hornblocks in the chassis using the coupling rods and London Road Models' tapered aluminium jigs as a positioning guide.

There is nothing more depressing than having to strip down a nearly completed chassis to put right a basic fault and I always try to get the potentially tricky parts of any model out of the way right at the start, so I don't have to go back to them. The next job, therefore, seemed to be to tackle the crossheads and slidebars. Finecast supply these in lost-wax brass, though cast nickel would look very well unpainted. They come in the usual tangle which has to be carefully sorted out. Are they cast like this, I wonder? Is there no way they can be supplied straight? These particular offerings are, unlike some, refreshingly accurate in terms of fit and, once the alignment was straightened out, needed only the minimum of easing with fine files for them to work as they should. The piston glands, cast integrally with the slidebars, hold the piston rods in place but I decided it would be better in engineering terms to have them sliding in brass tubes inside the cylinder. To achieve this I bored out the solid whitemetal cylinder castings and force-fitted into each a length of 1/8 in outside diameter tubing. Into this I slid successively smaller diameter tubes until they matched the diameter of the piston rod. We are not aiming, of course, to make this steam tight — a smooth sliding fit with no visible wobble is the end point.

Having soldered up the slidebar/piston rod assemblies, I tinned the backs of the glands with 145° solder and soldered them to the main casting using low-melt. For general whitemetal assembly I have used for many years a Litesold 50W iron specifically designed to work with low-melt solder, but here, because of the bulk of the castings, I used the quicker build-up of heat available from an ordinary 25W Antex. Once I had cleaned up the work with fine files and washed it in household cleaner to get rid of grit and flux residues, I dunked each assembly in Brasso and worked the crossheads by hand for a couple of minutes to get everything running silky-smooth. Again, there was no point in going any further until this desideratum had been achieved. Tight spots, in my experience, do not go away with time — if anything, they get worse. If you accumulate errors, then you are heading for disaster sooner rather than later. My approach is always to get every

The chassis is conventional to the point of tedium – beam compensation, MJT hornblocks, Romford gears and drivers. The D13 just happened to be lying around but it is perfectly adequate for such an application.

stage sorted out satisfactorily before moving onto the next.

The Finecast cylinders are designed, I suspect, for their A3 and are therefore not at all right for the Hush-Hush. The low-pressure outside cylinders — this engine was a compound — have a very visible outward bulge. Along with the locking wheel on the smokebox door, the cylinders are one of a number of curiously archaic-looking features on this most futuristic of steam locomotives, and help give it its distinctive character. To model the steam chests, I sawed out a strip of 10-thou brass and rolled it into a tight tube. I then cut off a couple of sections a centimetre or so in length and soldered them between the protruding cylinder covers to produce the required cylinder shape. Once the wheels are in place, the cylinders can be fixed to the chassis. Five-minute Bostik epoxy does very well here (I find it a much tougher adhesive than the equivalent Devcon or Araldite brands).

The motor I used was a D13, largely because it happened to be on hand and I had no other suitable use for it. A large express passenger locomotive seemed the ideal application because it is a powerful motor that is more comfortable running at speed than on slow shunting work and I didn't envisage seeing the Hush-Hush on Top End pilot duty too often. There is so much space inside its boiler, in fact, that anything up to the size of a Mashima 1833 would probably fit. The etched mount came from Finecast and the gears were Romford 40:1, a quieter set than usual. Although the small Ultrascale or Exactoscale gears and gearboxes suit my more diminutive prototypes superbly, I have a feeling that big engines, with the

vastly higher torque of their motors, ought to have big, grub-screw fitted gears. Is there, I wonder, any engineering truth in this impression? Or, in fitting the comparatively crude Romford gears to a selection of Pacifics and 4-6-0s, have I overlooked a more suitable alternative?

I used Romford wheels here, again because they were to hand — this time from a DJH A3 where I had preferred to use Alan Gibson products. Upgrading kits has an attendant cascading effect and it is nice sometimes to find a kit that will conveniently use up surplus fittings — as we will see in due course when we come to tackle the tender. The Romford driving wheels have two spokes too many, and, while they resemble no known prototype, they perhaps look more like Gresley-pattern wheels than anything else, especially when fitted with Kemilway axle-nut covers (long discontinued, but easy to pick up still) to represent the big central bosses. It was some time since I had last used Romford wheels and I was reminded of how easy they are to fit and adjust and, if necessary, to take off.

As with another notorious prototype, the Great Western 'Castle', clearances between driving wheel flanges on the Hush-Hush are minimal, and the proximity is accentuated when using wheels with overscale flanges. However, we still need to find an anchor point for the brake gear. I felt obliged to use .45mm wire to support the upper hangers as I don't think .33mm is quite man enough for the job. Getting the wire into the tube was no trouble but soldering it in place was an absolute swine. I have had some memorable tussles over the years when trying to obtain adequate clearances for valve gear,

brake shoes and suchlike, but soldering the brake hangers solidly on to the wheels was a new experience for me, even by my exalted standards of debauchery. In the end I took the wheels off, cleaned them up, soldered the wires in place and then refitted the wheels. I suppose I could always have fitted the wires first but, whenever I have done this in the past, I always seem to slash my fingers on them while fitting the wheels. Blood is the very devil to get out of gears and motors, I find. The Finecast brake gear is rudimentary and the diagram is extremely confusing — they show the front brake blocks forward of the wheels and *between* the frames — so I made my own linkages and cross-members from brass.

Once the half-built chassis could be coaxed into running along the test track in smooth and slinky fashion without too many shorts from the brake gear, I could turn to the front and rear bogies. These used the castings from the kit but I installed a system of side springing to guide the locomotive through curves. This engine has a considerable overhang front and rear and if it is effectively built as an 0-6-0, with the bogies merely coming along for the ride, it takes curves in a very awkward manner. The springing makes the transition much smoother and also stops the bogies flopping about all over the place when the loco is removed from the track.

The bodywork is cast in whitemetal, with a very small number of etched details. The castings are plain although, in truth, the Hush-Hush was not an especially 'detailed' locomotive. My main concern was for the accuracy of the two massive castings which form the outer casing and thus are the chief structural member of the bodywork. In a previous generation of whitemetal kits these would have been of two different lengths, with great thick moulding part lines and edges that refused to align. Finecast's offerings, however, are pretty good. They had, inevitably, become a little twisted somewhere along the way but because of the flexibility of the metal they could be straightened without difficulty. I soldered the rear bulkhead/spectacle plate to one half, checking that it was dead square, and the curved front cladding to the other and then united them with a generous fillet of solder along the top seam. I was pleasantly surprised to find that everything fitted together quite snugly, allowing for a tweak here and there to get the firebox side sheets to tuck under correctly and to ensure that the space underneath was square and parallel. I felt, however, that a couple of transverse bulkheads might not have come amiss both to strengthen the assembly and to ensure the correct profile is maintained. Under-boiler clearances for the chassis are designed for OO but are tightish for EM. To clear P4 wheels, as is usually the case with cast kits, quite a bit of metal will need to be cut away under the boiler, which is always a bore.

With its subtle curves and bulges, the boiler cladding of the Hush-Hush is an unfamiliar shape to most of us and it is difficult to recognise discrepancies. With the more familiar outline of a locomotive such as the A4, on the other hand, it is easy to see where planes and curves are not quite right, especially the distinctive 'hump'. Some pattern-makers seem to go to inordinate lengths to get the profile of their models wrong and so, for the builder, constant reference to drawings and photographs is necessary. Having soldered up the boiler cladding of the Hush-Hush, I compared the net result with profile photographs of the real thing and was well satisfied. Seen in side elevation, the lower firebox seems to slope a little too gently but this is an exceptionally difficult prototype and, generally speaking, Finecast's pattern-maker has done his job well here. I wonder what he was working from? I was unable to track down a decent scale drawing of the original Hush-Hush — though John Edgson has done the rebuilt W1 in his excellent Isinglass series — and so I based my modifications to the model on the 20 or so photographs of the locomotive that I was able to find in my library.

There is something very American about the outward appearance of the Hush-Hush. Parts of it remind me variously of the Union Pacific 4–4–4s and the streamlined New York Central Hudsons.

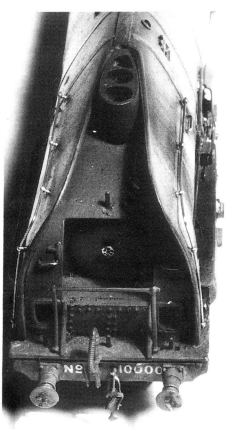

The front of the boiler cladding extends forwards to form a pair of smoke deflectors which I thinned down to half their former thickness and likewise the prominent lateral seam which runs along the top of the boiler benefited from a vigorous pass or six with the file. I also thinned down the edges of the cab sides and roof to make them look more like sheet metal than armour plate. I don't use proper files for white metal — except really big ones — because they clog too quickly and become useless. Instead I use ordinary emery board nail files, which cost pennies and do the job just as well.

Body detailing was a straightforward enough operation using the castings supplied. I went to work on the cab fittings, using the photograph in the RCTS *Locomotives of the LNER* as a guide, and I also made a few cosmetic improvements to the Cartazzi axleboxes and added the firebox damper rod and other details, like the pipes between engine and tender and all the running-plate gubbins above the cylinders. The Hush-Hush underwent a number of modifications over the years and one of the most visible alterations was made in 1934, when the 'telemotor' hydraulically-operated steam reverse was converted to screw operation. This made a big difference to the appearance of the left-hand running plate, although no provision is made for this in the kit (and yet the double chimney fitted in 1935 is included as an optional part). I did what I could with brass rod and tube, using photographs and the verbal description in the RCTS book as a guide. Mercifully a large extension plate bolted to the motion bracket hides the worst of it although I did make an attempt to model the weighshaft and other visible details.

The motion comes in the form of an etched nickel silver fret. I don't know whether I was having an off day, for I didn't get on with this terribly well although I have built enough locomotives with outside Walschaerts gear over the years. I found the radius rod and the union link were both approximately 2mm too long and needed correcting. The whole etch had a chunky look to it. While the coupling and connecting rods on the prototype are substantial forgings, the use of high-tensile steels in certain parts of the valve gear on Gresley locomotives imparted quite a delicate look to the motion. Dave Bradwell's B1 chassis kit and the Finney A3 evoke this characteristic rather well but, with the Hush-Hush, the only way to capture this essential feature was by extensive thinning of the relevant components — the eccentric rod, radius rod, combination lever and union link. In some cases I gave up and made the components myself out of nickel etch waste.

One of my main reservations about the kit concerned the tender. Quite apart from the distinctive GNR design with coal rails, there were three separate families of Gresley eight-wheeled tender, superficially similar but with many detail differences when studied closely. As built, the Hush-Hush had a corridor tender (number 5484) of similar design to those attached originally to members of the A1/A3 class, with a flat back panel (later ones, built exclusively for the A4s, were bow-ended) and flush sides. Tender No. 5484, however, was unique among the 1929 batch in having disc rather than spoked wheels and, to match the cab sides on the locomotive, being almost a foot wider (7ft 10in) across the inward curves of the front side sheets. When it was rebuilt into streamlined form the W1 retained this corridor tender but in May 1948 it was exchanged for the non-corridor, streamline tender from an A4, *William Whitelaw*. The original Hush-

Hush tender, rather surprisingly, survives to this day because, when *William Whitelaw* was withdrawn, tender No. 5484 passed to *Union of South Africa* which had been bought for preservation but whose own corridor tender had already been acquired for conversion to an auxiliary water tender for *Flying Scotsman*. Though I knew nothing of its history, and little suspected that, 30 years later, I would make a model of it, I well remember scrambling through *Union of South Africa*'s 'new' corridor tender when the engine was stored at Thornton, prior to delivery to the Lochty Private Railway.

The Finecast Hush-Hush has a corridor tender but, even in the photograph on the box, the sides look a scale six inches too low and its width is quite wrong. Gresley corridor tenders were 8ft 9in wide and the side sheets were flush with the other edges of the floor. The Finecast tender body, however, is much skinnier and has the pronounced ledge characteristic of the 'New Type' and streamlined tenders fitted to most of the Gresley Pacifics, whose tanks were barely 8ft wide. Once again, I suspect, accuracy has been sacrificed in the name of expediency. The tender supplied with the Hush-Hush appears to marry the sides of a New Type tender with the rear panel from the original corridor design, and the result is neither one thing nor t'other.

I wasn't too struck by the general appearance of the tender either, with all those exposed whitemetal edges a scale three inches thick — it looked like a 20-year-old piece of pattern making, not at all the kind of fine work we have become accustomed to in recent years from people like Adrian Swain and DJH. My solution was to ignore the Finecast castings altogether and to use instead some etched brass components from the DJH A3 kit. This might seem like a reckless extravagance but in fact there is sound common sense to it. DJH, at least, seem to have realised that were sufficient major differences between the Gresley tender types to warrant separate kits for each, although certain components are shared and are consequently not duplicated. They produce two versions of the A1/A3, one with the GNR tender alone and another, which I have, which includes a large number of alternative tender parts for the New Type, streamlined and corridor variants. At no extra cost to myself, these spare parts formed the basis of the new tender for the Hush-Hush.

Having set aside the etched components that I would need for a New Type tender for *Blink Bonny*, there was enough left over to make most of a correctly-proportioned corridor tender for the Hush-Hush — the sides, rear, corridor connection, coal space with corridor roof, tender front and rear bulkhead, together with a few other bits and pieces, were all conveniently to hand. Because they have a different profile to the other types, the

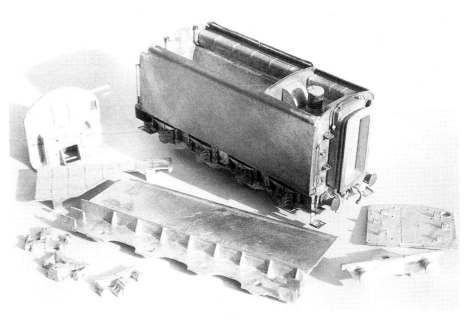

I made the tender out of spare parts from a DJH A3, with a little improvisation.

spare set of side sheets from the DJH kit — intended for the streamlined tender — needed a little filing to create the correct outline, but otherwise all I had to make from scratch were the tender side frames and floor, the side and rear steps, right-hand side coal rail, tender filler and dome. I used axlebox castings from ABS (ref. L400) and fabricated the rest myself, using 10-thou brass for the underframe, riveted with a Graskop rivet punch. I retained the etched tender chassis and brake gear from the Finecast kit but cut the side frames down to a depth of 11mm to obtain the correct ride height. The extra width at the front of the tender was achieved by simply not bending the side sheets round so much.

Finecast's instructions suggest the loco be finished with grey aerosol car primer. This is the way their demonstration model that they take to exhibitions is painted and it looks very well. However I suspect this is not at all the 'dark battleship grey' to which contemporary sources refer. Grey primer looks, in a black and white photograph, very like the 'works grey' in which many locomotives, the Hush-Hush included, have traditionally been paraded for the camera. Photographs of the Hush-Hush at work and, crucially, on public display suggest a much darker colour; even in the 1930s, when the paintwork would have lightened somewhat, it still doesn't look much like grey primer to me. My chosen colour therefore was Humbrol gloss Dark Grey, No. 5. It may be just as inaccurate but I have a hunch that it is nearer the mark. According to the RCTS *Locomotives of the LNER* the buffer beams were also unrelieved grey, though Finecast suggest they be painted red. Studying the available photographs, I came out on the side of the RCTS. I had modelled the locomotive in the latter years of its short life and it is lightly weathered to suggest an engine that is no longer the apple of the running department's eye.

I scraped away the paint to reveal bare metal which represents the polished boiler bands. This is very Odeonesque and I was so pleased by the result that, with a sudden rush of blood to the head, I decided to use stainless steel numbering and lettering to enhance the effect. The Hush-Hush had 12in white characters, shaded black, which I felt looked rather dated in comparison with the Art Deco styling and painting of the locomotive. As a piece of self-indulgence totally at variance with

the finescale credo, I used etched 'stainless steel' letter forms from CGW, designed for the A4s, which I thought were much more à la mode. I am sure the style-conscious Gresley would have used them if they had been available to him at the time — they only came into general use in 1935, when time was running out for the Hush-Hush. The numbers on the buffer beam came from that very useful sheet of transfers that comes with Slater's PO wagons. As a footnote, the W1 never carried a name in either incarnation although it is understood that straight-pattern *British Enterprise* nameplates were cast for it but never fitted, 'perhaps fortunately as things turned out', as the RCTS account has it. They would have been mounted, unusually, on the firebox sides of the Hush-Hush.

In most of the twenty or so views that I have of the Hush-Hush, the engine is very smartly turned out. It was obviously regarded as something special but, towards the end, its appearance was a little run down. I weathered the model in accordance with a photograph of the prototype taken at Neville Hill in its final months — by then, it is starting to look neglected, as though official patience is running thin. The paintwork is stained and there is a lot of oil and dust about on exposed surfaces. I also had in mind one or two shots I have seen of silver-grey A4s looking none too clean. Basic weathering was a heavily diluted wash of Humbrol matt leather (No. 62) and Metalcote gunmetal sloshed over the whole of the engine and tender, most of which was promptly wiped and dabbed off with brushes, tissues and cotton buds, generally working downwards to suggest streaking but sometimes done with a circular motion to simulate the cleaner's rag. Each pass with a different tool creates a different effect, subtly enhancing the general discolouration. I airbrushed a sooty deposit around the chimney and running back to the cab roof, and then got to work with Carr's weathering powders, building up accumulated deposits of grot around the axleboxes, the smokebox door and among the paraphernalia of the running plate. The final act was to coal the tender with some pretty rubbishy stuff, to suggest more signs of growing indifference to the Hush-Hush and all its manifold problems.

So there we have it — an impressive and highly unusual locomotive that is slightly bigger than a Princess Royal and a good six scale feet longer than a

Britannia. I doubt if I shall use it so very often but that was not the point of the exercise. To sum up — a useful kit if one is prepared to do a lot of work on it but otherwise, especially in comparison with other recent Finecast offerings, a bit of a throwback. Ten years ago I would have thought it was pretty good — despite the major problem with the tender, the loco parts at least fitted very well and the castings capture the character of the locomotive with considerable subtlety, which was certainly not true of the average whitemetal kit on which I cut my finescale modelling teeth. With hindsight, I might have preferred to buy in or build a more accurate chassis and valve gear set, but this would have left me with another load of more or less useless bits and pieces — I am sure one day I will build a kit using none of the original components. Still, full credit to Finecast for tackling such a prototype — I hope it's sold well enough to justify their investment. May we hope that, one day, an equally unlikely kit, the Bulleid 'Leader', might come along as well? At least there were five of them, even if only two were ever finished and just one actually ran — which, when I think about it, sounds a bit like my collection of kits.

LNER CONTAINER FLAT, 7mm

Adapting the Gibson RCH underframe kit, by DERYCK FEATHERSTONE

On a visit to Alan Gibson's workshop I saw a made-up example of his kit for a 7mm scale RCH steel wagon underframe and was tempted to buy one. I didn't particularly want yet another RCH wagon but it seemed to me that it might form the basis for some other type of steel-framed vehicle. My favoured Great Eastern, for example, was an early user of steel underframes. It is relatively easy to build a wooden underframe from plastic sheet or even wood itself, but channel solebars call for a different approach and rather more time, especially if small detail, such as bolt heads, are to be added.

The Gibson solebars have etched lines to allow 16ft and 16ft 6in length wagons to be made by trimming the 7ft 6in ones provided, and there are also 9ft and 10ft wheel-base versions – therefore, plenty of choice. Unfortunately the GER used a 9ft 6in wheelbase for its 'normal' wagons, which meant such major surgery that it did not seem worthwhile. Eventually, I decided on an LNER 'Conflat' as being a quick and easy job which would enable me to evaluate the kit without too much alteration; it was also a wagon I needed.

The wagon chosen was LNER No. 163677 which is shown in plates 145 and 155 in Peter Tatlow's classic *Pictorial Record of LNER Wagons* (OPC 1976). This was an earlier 9ft WB version which preceded the more common 10ft 'Conflat S' which was built in large numbers right into BR days.

The basic underframe assembled easily with my resistance soldering unit and calls for little comment. I dispensed with the compensation as I do not find it necessary for short-wheelbase wagons. Gibson wheelsets were used – the Slater's ones would, I found, require shortened axles to fit. There's little to choose in appearance between these makes but it is often better not to mix the breed. Buffers are not supplied and the instructions rightly explain that this is because so many different types were used. I had a suitable set of long-bodied, sprung ones in stock which look identical to those in the photos. I used a set of lost-wax screw couplings (I'm not sure whose); they are somewhat over-scale but better, I think, than the etched ones.

The kit provides a variety of types of brakegear, single or both sides independent, Moreton and four-shoe vacuum, but, of course, my wagon had to have the full eight-shoe vacuum set! I had a set of ABS whitemetal gear in stock, LNER type and 9ft wheelbase. The ABS brake hangers are in one casting of two-to-each-wheel and required quite a lot of carving to get them to fit round the W-irons, but they did provide a bit of much needed weight. I retained the Gibson etches for the V-hangers, pin racks and brake levers (shortened)

as I don't like the thick ABS whitemetal ones, or even the plastic ones still supplied by some manufacturers.

The brake gear rigging was corrected by the addition of drop links outside the wheelbase, as described in my MRJ review of the Connoisseur LNER 'Lowfit' kit. It would be better to solder these to the floor before fitting the wheels – I didn't, and it wasn't easy. If the wagon floor is plastic or wood, the drop-links could be pinned or Araldited to it.

The wagon body couldn't have been simpler and consisted of a sheet of 0.35mm brass for the floor, two sides of 3mm brass angle, a few wooden battens and two bearers of 3mm × 1mm channel section (I bought the latter some years ago and was delighted to find a use for it at last). Along the top of the sides were a series of holes to take shackles, 16 in all, for the securing chains for different sizes of containers. The holes were drilled with a 0.7mm drill and the shackles, which seemed to have been permanently fitted, were made with thin brass pins and 10 amp fuse wire. The pins were from a haberdashery store and had shanks 0.55mm diameter and heads only about 1.2mm. I think they were intended for lacemaking, so look in

at one of these shops – you'll be surprised how many potential modelling aids you will find! The wire was looped tightly round the pin and fixed with a touch of solder. The pin was pushed through the hole and the wire was looped over a 1mm rod and again twisted and soldered to the pin. Trimmed up, they looked quite convincing.

With all the whitemetal and plastic kits plus specialised etched ones, where does Alan Gibson's underframe fit in? Apart from the ubiquitous minerals, steel underframes to RCH specifications were used for a variety of wagons, vans and tanks for the LNER, LMS and private owners, and many were perpetuated almost unchanged into BR, so this kit is a useful aid to scratchbuilding those not available in kit form. The Conflat convinces me that it is capable of further adaptation. However, at about £10 plus wheels and buffers, let alone any substitutions such as different brakegear or couplings, it should not be regarded as a cheap option. Whatever finished wagon one ends up with, the total cost is not likely to be much different from that of a complete kit for a similar wagon. As a scratchbuilder's aid, I consider it of good quality and reasonable value.

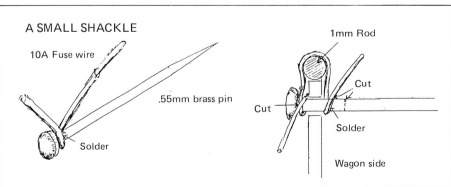

A SMALL SHACKLE

10A Fuse wire

Solder

.55mm brass pin

1mm Rod

Cut

Cut

Solder

Wagon side

GWR '517' IN P4

STEPHEN WILLIAMS builds and improves an Alan Gibson kit:

For modellers of the Great Western, the '517' class 0-4-2 tank engines are most useful. The prototype was introduced as early as 1868 and a further 12 lots were constructed between then and 1885, by which time almost 150 engines were in service. Many lasted well into the 1930s when they were generally replaced by Collett's 48XX class 0-4-2 tanks, engines which were visibly a reworking of Armstrong's original design. Their light axle loading meant they could work anywhere on the system — which is more or less what they did!

I needed a '517' for my model of Faringdon. Although other small engines worked the Faringdon branch, the '517' tanks were a mainstay in and around the period in which my model is set, and the layout would not look quite right until one was in service. Two options were available — an etched kit from Blacksmith or a cast and etched kit from Alan Gibson. The Gibson kit is a re-issue (with improvements) of an old M & L kit. I already have an M & L kit for the '633' class 0-6-0T working the layout which, although devoid of fine detail, looks the part and runs well. So I opted for the Gibson kit to provide me with at least the basis for the model, which I could embellish as necessary. In the end, the embellishments rather took over, but the result is, I feel, a pleasing model of a characterful prototype.

The '517s' are not, however, an easy group to model. With a construction phase that extended over 15 years and a service life on many engines in excess of 50 years, there were lots of changes to individuals within the class. Most, though not all, were built with a 15ft wheelbase and, whilst some had inside bearings to the trailing wheels, others had outside bearings. Through time, most seem to have been converted to outside bearings on the trailing wheels, but this was not universal. Round-topped fireboxes were generally replaced by Belpaire versions but cab and bunker combinations varied between the Collett extended bunker and enclosed cab to the open half-cab and flat-backed bunker — and any of the permutations in between!

The placement of smaller fittings such as the fillers, vents and tool boxes on the tank tops seem to have been similarly prone to almost random variation. So, photographs of your chosen engine are highly desirable.

The Faringdon engine I wanted to model was No. 839. Indeed, I had a pair of number-plates especially etched by Gordon Watford as long ago as 1980 in anticipation, but to this date I have not come across a photo of No. 839 at any period, let alone circa 1922. The closest I have got are Nos. 835 and 837. With '517' class engines there is absolutely no guarantee that numerical proximity signifies similarity in style, but in the end I had to assume that 839 would have looked like these two. Both had Belpaire fireboxes (as I would expect by the 1920s) and both had inside bearings on the trailing wheels and half cabs. No. 835 was photographed around 1926 and had an extended bunker, but, for my period, the flat-backed bunker sported by No. 837 is more likely to have been correct. The arrangement of the smaller fittings on the two engines was generally consistent. So that was the combination I decided to model.

I must admit that initially my hope had been that Alan Gibson's kit would give me what I needed without too much extra effort. I have no doubts that an adequate model of a '517' engine can be built from the kit as supplied, but having spent the last two or three years working on Finney and Mitchell kits, I have become more attuned to points of detail. I have to say, too, that as I progressed through the project, I found one or two rather obvious faults in the design which, in all honesty, could not be rectified using the parts supplied. Of these the most serious was the casting for the bunker which, in the kit I had purchased, actually proved to be wider than the footplate! Lesser sources of irritation included splasher tops that were too narrow and a rather strange bevelling of the tank sides where they joined the tops. I presume this was done to reduce the effect of thickness within the edge of the cast-

ing, but when viewed from above (as models tend to be) it looks quite wrong. So some scratchbuilding seemed desirable and, in the case of the bunker, inevitable. Set against these negative aspects, however, were some excellent lost-wax castings which gave me encouragement that it wasn't all going to be an uphill struggle.

CHASSIS

I started assembly with the chassis. The main-frames are etched from some stout nickel silver and allow for either a rigid, sprung or — with a little extra work — a compensated chassis. For a P4 model I wanted an active chassis but I'm not a great fan of sprung systems of the type supplied in the kit, so I opted for compensation. I then had to decide on the arrangement, the simplest configuration seemingly being to drive the leading axle and allow the compensation beam to work on the trailing driving axle and the trailing wheels. This would pose some slight problems in accommodating the motor (I had chosen a Portescap 1219 to power this engine), but I felt these could be overcome.

The frames have no provision for a beam system of compensation, so it is important to work this out before assembly begins and everything is still flat and easy to work upon. The simplest way to do this is to mount one wheel onto each axle and temporarily position these into one of the frames. This permits you to mark out where the pivot should be located to allow the chassis to stand naturally level, although obviously this can be adjusted later if things aren't quite right, by gentle bending of the beam. I tack-soldered the two frames together and drilled through at the marked point. Whilst the frames were still together, I used my piercing saw to open up the two slots for the moving axles and ensured that the fixed bearing could be properly located, too. Then I separated the frames and cleaned it all up.

The frames include a representation of the bottom of the firebox and ashpan, but I noticed whilst I had the wheels temporarily positioned that this was too short. On the prototype the firebox/ashpan extended behind the trailing wheels whereas on the model it stopped short. Close inspection of photographs of '517' class engines also showed that the detailing on this, as represented in the kit, wasn't anything like the real thing. These aren't difficult faults to rectify, the existing firebox being simply cut away (following the line of the frames) and a new one, cut from 10-thou nickel silver, substituted. I took the opportunity to use my Tony Reynalds riveting tool (the only Reynalds I'm ever likely to be able to afford!) to emboss the line of rivets which I could see on the prototype. After the new pieces were soldered in place, I used some scrap brass from the etching fret to add the little brackets where the firebox met the line of the frames.

Then the frames were assembled onto the spacers to form the basic chassis. I would have liked a little more help from the kit in the alignment of frames and spacers — some proper tabs and slots for example. But with careful work involving the engineer's square, it went together correctly and without too much difficulty.

The compensation components I had purchased from London Road Models, who provide all the bits you need — bearings, guides, wire and tube for the beam and pivot. I have never had any difficulty in assembling a compensated chassis, provided one is careful and follows some simple basic rules. First, with a round needle file (or a reamer), open out the bearing hole to accept the axle. You don't want any slop but neither should there be even a hint of tightness of bearing on axle. The test I use is a simple one — as soon as the bearing will drop off the axle under gravity alone, then it's time to stop. Then secondly, the bearing guides must be cleaned up to the point at which the bearings move smoothly within the guides and without (this is important) any discernible lateral movement. The gravity test, once again, is a good guide to when the cleaning work has reached the right stage. I like to keep pairings of guides and bearings together once they are matched, and if, like the London Road bearings, they are square, it is a good idea to mark the top of the bearing with a dot of paint. Sometimes a bearing that is apparently a good fit in the guide will not work as well if it becomes inverted or reorientated during assembly. The spot of paint helps us get this right.

To attach the bearing guides to the frames, we need first to have a pair of matched coupling rods. The Gibson kit provides both fluted and plain rods but both sets need to be laminated together to get a decent thickness, ensuring that the correct pattern is on the outer

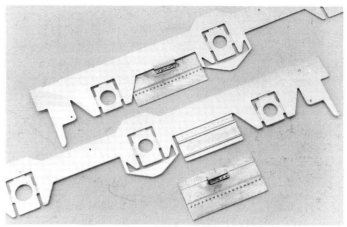

The locomotive main-frames, as supplied (centre), and with the modified frames (above). On the real engines, the firebox and ashpan were longer than shown in the kit and sported a prominent bracket. The replacement part for the second unmodified frame is shown at the bottom.

The mainframes have been assembled and the hornblock guides are here shown being positioned. The front axle is in a fixed driving position and the compensation is provided by movement on the second driving wheels and the trailing axle. Note how the coupling rods act as spacing jigs for correct positioning of the guides which are held temporarily by the coil spring through which the second axle is threaded. The photograph also shows the pivot for the compensating beam as well as the cross wires for the brake hangers.

face (for my engine, plain rods were more likely to be correct). Next, I tack-soldered the two rods together, being as careful as possible that they were correctly aligned one with the other. Then I was able to drill out the crankpin holes to match the pins and be confident that the coupling rods, once separated, would be identical.

The coupling rods provide the means for precise positioning of the bearing guides. I have some Perseverance assembly jigs that help with this task — ⅛ in steel rods which match the axle diameters but with extended ends turned down to match the crankpins. One of these rods goes through the fixed bearing at the front and then a pair of bearings and their guides are threaded onto the second axle with a strong spring between them. This is slid into place between the frames, the pressure of the spring being sufficient to hold it all in position. The coupling rods are then placed over the extended parts of the two rods and the vertical alignment of the bearing guides given a final check before being soldered in place. This method should ensure a chassis with a precise wheelbase that ought (in consequence) to run smoothly.

To find out how smoothly, we must mount the motor and wheels. I had in stock some Ultrascale wheels (which I view as quite simply the best and which I always use on my engines provided the right pattern is available), so I used the wheels supplied in the kit to set

the chassis up and then substituted the Ultrascales when it was all working. Modellers occasionally get into a pickle over quartering wheels, but it really isn't difficult if a simple system is followed, especially with a four-coupled chassis. Start with the driven axle and, using the spokes as guides, align the two wheels by eye with the cranks in something like the right position (on GWR engines, the right-hand side, when looking forward from the cab, usually leads by 90 degrees). Lock these wheels in place with Loctite 601, once you are satisfied — not forgetting to locate your gear box/set first! — then take the second axle, mount one wheel in place and lock that one, too. Mark this one with a spot of paint for identification purposes since the basic principle is that none of the wheels fixed so far is to be moved again. Now, using the spokes as a visual guide, mount the final wheel onto its axle as close as possible to what you judge to be the correct position. Fit the coupling rod to the wheels on the opposite side and then offer up the rod to the side to which you have just added the fourth wheel. If the rod won't go over the crankpins, carefully adjust the position of the last wheel until it does. You should now have a perfectly quartered chassis which you can test on the track under finger power and, when all is well, lock the final wheel in place.

As the photographs show (just!) I like to make a little mount for Portescap motors.

The basic chassis, ready to be wired and tested. The motor is taped to a small bracket fixed between the frames and the photograph also shows the compensating beam mounted on its pivot. Notice how the beam is cranked downwards to bear on the trailing axle which has a lower midpoint than the driving wheel. Adjustments to make the locomotive sit level are achieved simply by bending this section of the beam up or down, as required.

Some kit designers seem quite happy to have these units untethered, but I have a theory that running can be affected by the mass of the motor moving around inside the boiler or firebox. So where possible, I add a simple bracket from 10-thou nickel silver that is soldered between the frames. The motor is attached to the bracket with a length of masking tape so removal, if necessary, is quite easy.

Alan Gibson includes sprung plunger pickups for power collection although my preference is for phosphor-bronze wires bearing onto the edges of the wheel flanges. I find these easier to adjust and it's also easier to see when one of them isn't doing the job it is supposed to do! To accommodate these, I soldered a piece of nickel silver between the frames near the bottom of the new firebox/ashpan assembly. Copper-clad Paxolin strips were then glued to this piece with Loctite, and wire pick-ups to each of the six wheels soldered to these strips. The motor terminals were then connected to each strip and the moment of truth arrived — a powered test. In this case the chassis behaved immaculately.

Once you have a chassis that works to your complete satisfaction, the trick thereafter is to ensure that nothing you do disturbs the mechanism that you have worked carefully to set up. However, there is still quite a bit to do in the way of detailing, starting with the brake hangers.

I'm afraid the kit lets itself down again with the brakes. The exploded diagram shows the correct arrangement with the brake shoes sandwiched between pairs of hangers. However, the parts supplied don't allow you to do this, as there are only four hangers rather than the requisite eight. The distinctive asymmetrical shape of the hanger is not captured either. For some reason that I now cannot fathom, I used the parts supplied but it doesn't look right and I suspect I will have to return to the problem in due course. I do find design faults like these brakes annoying. I presume these are new parts that were prepared for the revised kit and it's just as easy to do it right as it is to do it wrong!

Prototype photographs show sundry plumbing and pipework that needs to be added to give the chassis a look of completion. There is some kind of ejector attached to the right-hand firebox/ashpan casing which I cobbled together from scraps of brass wire, and I also included sanding pipes. These were bent up from 0.7mm wire and soldered into notches cut into the very tops of the frames. In this way they

look like they are descending from the sandboxes above the footplate whereas, in practice, they are integral with the chassis.

Lastly, on the chassis, I fitted the balance weights to the driving wheels. On the real '517s' these usually had a distinct pattern of rivets although the etched parts in the kit were quite plain. No matter, a few minutes spent marking positions and a couple of minutes

Underside view of the chassis prior to fitting pick-ups. The copper-clad Paxolin strip to which the phosphor-bronze pick-ups are soldered shows clearly.

Left-hand side of the completed chassis, with brakes, balance weights and rear sanding pipes now in place.

with the Reynalds riveter set that right without too much difficulty, and that was the chassis ready for final painting. Notice from the photographs that the main part of the chassis was painted before final assembly of the wheels — it is much easier to do this at an early stage rather than trying to poke brushes loaded with paint between the spokes and around all the extras.

BODY

I started the body assembly with preparation of the footplate — embossing the line of rivets around the leading edge and soldering fixing nuts over the two holes provided for bolting the chassis to the body. The positions of the rivets are given on the underside by half-etched locating marks of truly awesome proportions. Quite why such large indentations have been used (and they are the same size on all the etched parts that require rivets to be embossed) I am not sure. But if you are building one of these kits, please don't punch through the entire locating mark, otherwise you will end up with rivet heads of a size found on an ocean liner! I set my riveting tool up carefully so that just a small part of the centre of each locating mark was embossed, and it produced a very fine effect.

A close-up of the front buffer beam with the first sets of rivets having just been formed. To create the rivet patterns accurately, it is essential that the rivet punch is very carefully positioned within the unnecessarily large half-etched locating points on the reverse. This applies to all the rivets in the kit that the modeller has to form.

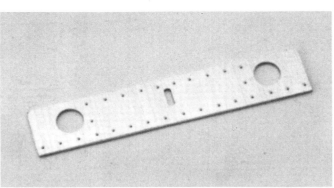

Next I tackled the front splashers. These are tricky and I'm afraid you don't get much help from the instructions which, throughout the assembly, are terse. I started by folding up the face of the little coupling rod boss splasher (which is set within the main wheel splasher) and reinforced this with a fillet of solder on the inside. Then I positioned the main splasher faces. Trial-and-error deduced that this perches on the very edge of the footplate cut-out, not set within the cut-out, and in the absence of anything to help with location, this is a difficult join to make. I had to do some unsoldering here but in the end I managed to get it into the right position and set vertically.

The splasher top for the coupling rod boss unit doesn't fit — it's too long and too narrow — so I cut a piece of thin nickel-silver sheet to approximately the right shape, formed a curve by gentle rolling with a brass rod on a soft surface (a computer mouse mat is good for this) and worked it into the right position. I think this needs to make a butt joint flush with the inside of the splasher face, not resting on its top. At this stage it doesn't matter if this piece extends beyond the inner face of the main splasher as this can be filed away once the part is secure. I tack-soldered the part first and, once I was happy that it looked all right, completed the seams and cleaned away any excess metal and/or solder. Then I repeated the process with the tops for the main splashers. Here I used the part supplied although, once again, it is several millimetres too long. I recommend removing any excess before the splasher top is fitted and, as before, I attached the top behind the face, flush with the edge.

Next, I fitted the valances and buffer beams. The valances carry a few rivets (as do the buffer beams) so more careful work with the riveting tool was needed first. Then using a square, I soldered the front buffer beam in place, to be followed by the two footplate valances and lastly the rear buffer beam. The correct alignment for the footplate valances is indicated merely with some half-etched lines on the underside, so builders have to be very careful that everything is straight and evenly spaced from the footplate edge. I do feel that Alan has missed an opportunity with this engine. A kit of this type ought to be an ideal beginner's project, but little weaknesses in the design — parts that don't quite fit or, as here, parts that have to be located without any anchorage points — really mean that it's a model only suited to someone with experience. I managed to fit these valances without too much trouble by using pieces of Blu-tak to provide temporary fixing and by tack-soldering and checking before putting solder right along the join. But I can see modellers getting into a mess and, with a little more thought at the design stage, such problems could surely be minimised.

Since parts of the main body superstructure are mostly whitemetal, I decided to fit as many of the small footplate details that needed

Early stages of work on the footplate. The locating bolts have been soldered in place and the unit tested to ensure there is no fouling of the wheels or rods. The problemmatic front splashers are in place, as is the front buffer beam, but none of the other footplate detail.

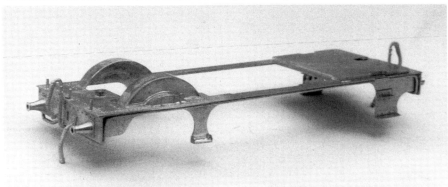

The footplate after detailing — essentially the fitting of steps, buffers, lamp irons, steam and vacuum hoses and the prominent piping that ran along the valance. Detail such as the valance pipes are not mentioned in the kit instructions or supplied as components, but this kind of detail is easy to add using odd lengths of wire.

soldering at this point, rather than risk working with a hot iron around castings that would easily melt.

The steps came next, the etched parts being simple fold-up jobs that solder into recesses in the valance (for the cab), or which fit around the main vertical support for the forward step on the valance. However, the photographs of prototypes show that the cab steps had fixing rivets on their backplates, so after the step was folded, but before it was fixed, the riveting tool was called back into play (the Reynalds riveter has a special extended doll which allows you to emboss step rivets after the metal is folded — a most useful device).

Then I fitted the vacuum and steam hoses and the lamp brackets. The hoses come as neat lost-wax brass castings and these are easily soldered in place on the buffer beams once they have been cleaned up with fine files and the fibreglass pencil. The lamp brackets, however, are a problem. The kit supplies etchings to form the distinctive offset pattern of lamp bracket that the GWR fitted to its rear bunkers, but the front brackets were not generally of this style, photographs showing most engines fitted with a simple angle fitting. Even if the cranked designs were correct, there aren't enough in the kit to do front and back, so I hunted amongst the etched fret for a thin strip that had been left over from removing another part and used this to fashion some new brackets for the front. Five lengths of about 4mm are needed, each folded into a simple, equal right-angle and then sweated into place (GWR modellers should remember that this style of bracket was usually offset so that an attached lamp would rest in the correct position). Three brackets go across the front edge of the footplate, and two (for spare lamps) are positioned alongside the wheel splasher on the left-hand side only — again, when viewing the engine from the cab.

With most of the footplate detail in place, I turned my attention to the main superstructure. The kit instructions which hitherto had been concise (to a fault) now become even more economical, so I followed my own sequence. I was confused, intially, about the role of a piece of flat milled brass which I found in the bottom of the kit box until I realised it was meant to provide the raised cab floor. This part has two holes drilled in it, one to locate a brake standard and the other to clear the rear fixing nut. However, to achieve the latter, it is necessary to drill this hole out substantially before it will fit. There is absolutely no guidance on where this part is to be located (and only by careful scrutiny of the exploded diagram does one discover on which side the brake standard is fitted) so I went for some guesswork. Each side has a milled notch which I assumed should be aligned with the topmost cab step, which is what I did. I think this is correct because when I offered up one of the cast bunkers (the kit is good in providing you with three alternative designs) it fitted neatly around this brass plate

A close-up of the new tank top, cut from 10-thou nickel silver. I realised after this photograph was taken that one of the sets of holes (for lifting rings) was in the wrong place, so some patching and re-drilling became necessary!

The engine with the cast tank sides and the new nickel-silver tank top in place.

and at the correct position relative to the rear buffer beam.

The first castings added were the tank sides. I said earlier that these have a rather exaggerated bevel where they meet the tank top, but the sides themselves are entirely acceptable, with good crisp rivet pattern and virtually no flash. There was some slight surface roughness, but that came out easily with a little work from the fibreglass pencil. My solution to the problem of the bevel was going to be to cut a new tank top from nickel silver sheet that would rest a little higher and hide the bevel effect, so the cleaned sides were soldered carefully in place on the footplate in order that the dimensions of the new top could be accurately measured. (To solder whitemetal to brass, first tin the brass with a thin layer of ordinary solder. The special 70° whitemetal solder will take quite happily to this, especially if you use plenty of flux — but don't dwell with the iron or you do risk meltdown of the part you are

soldering, even on quite big castings such as the tank sides. If in doubt, use an adhesive.)

With the tank sides in place, I could now work out the shape for the new tank top. Notice that this has not just to clear the Portescap motor, but also to provide a suitable cut-out for the etched cab front/side assembly. I couldn't find a clear view of the tank top of a '517', but pictures of later engines seemed to suggest that the top was only set a little way below the sides, so I cut a shape that would sit about 1mm below the top of the sides. For the record, the dimensions of the shape I cut are given in *Fig. 1*, but if you are following this with a '517' of your own, the figures might be slightly different, depending upon small variations in the positioning of the tank sides or, more probably, the motor that you are using if it is not a Portescap 1219. Before the top was attached to the sides, I marked and drilled out locating holes for the tank fillers and vents and also for some lifting rings. I don't know, for a

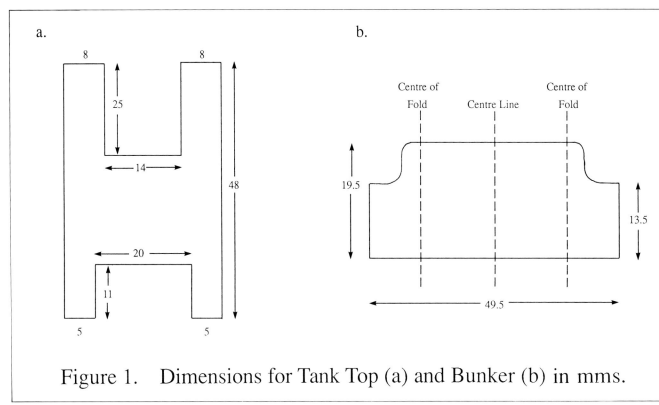

Figure 1.   Dimensions for Tank Top (a) and Bunker (b) in mms.

fact, that '517's had lifting rings on their tanks, but most GWR tank engines did, including the offspring of the '517', the Collett 48XX class, so I drilled a set of holes to allow these to be fitted a bit later. Once I was satisfied that all was as it should be, I soldered the top to the tank sides and filled the slight gap around the edge (a consequence of the bevelled edge on the tank side casting) with Milliput.

The kit casting for the tank top also includes the boiler top. My modifications therefore required that I find a new boiler, since the parts supplied in the kit would sit too high on the now-raised tank top. As it happens, I would have had to do this anyway as the Portescap motor on the front axle fouls the inside of the cast boiler barrel, whereas a thin-walled brass tube has just enough clearance to fit around the motor.

Fortunately, I found some brass tubing of exactly the right diameter in a K&S Metal Centre display that most model shops keep these days, although I could have made six boilers from the piece I had to buy! I squared-off one end by careful work with a flat file and then marked out the dimensions for the new boiler. It is obviously important to ensure that the new boiler matches precisely the size and configuration of the old one, so, to help me get this right, I used the cast boiler sections to make a paper template which I then glued around the new brass tube with a few spots of Evo-stik. The various cut-outs were then made around this template with the piercing saw and cleaned with files before the paper template was removed. The glue comes away easily from the brass with a few wipes of abrasive

Close-up of the new bunker and boiler. The new bunker was neces-- sary because the cast item provided in the kit didn't fit the footplate but the need for a new boiler was prompted by the selection of a Portescap motor which created impossibly tight clearances if I had retained the cast boiler provided in the kit.

paper. The centre line of the boiler was then carefully marked and the locating hole for the dome drilled out.

Once I was satisfied that the new boiler was a perfect fit, I added the boiler bands. These were cut with a Stanley knife from thin copper foil and sweated into place with 145° solder. The cast smokebox needs to be drilled for the chimney and marked along its centre line, after which the boiler and smokebox were carefully soldered together, using the centre lines to achieve the correct alignment of parts. At critical junctures such as this it is always a good

idea to check things most thoroughly before proceeding. I thought, at the time, that I had got things correctly lined up and it was only much later (and after I couldn't do much about it) that I discovered a slight misalignment — fortunately one that is only just apparent from one or two angles.

With the boiler and smokebox in place, I then turned my attention to the bunker and cab. The new bunker was cut from a sheet of 10-thou nickel silver. I have set out the dimensions that I used in *Fig. 1* and to satisfy myself that these would fit, I spent five minutes making a dummy bunker from thin card, before I set to work with the metal. The rivets — along the base of the bunker and up the middle of the back where, on the prototype, the two sheets were joined — were carefully embossed, and then, using a rubber mat and carefully applying pressure with a brass rod, the corners were formed. The beading along the top of the bunker was added with fuse wire, stripped of its coating with some fine abrasive paper and then carefully sweated into place with a minimum of 145° solder. Last of all, I drilled locating holes for the cabside handrails and the three hooks for the fire irons, before carefully soldering the new bunker to the footplate. I retained the cast bunker front which fitted quite happily, with just a little Milliput to fill the gap created by the use of the thinner material for the new bunker.

The distinctive half-cab also required some additional work before it could be fitted. The etched part supplied in the kit had simple semicircular cut-outs in the side sheets, but Swindon — or Wolverhampton in this case — was seldom so obvious in its design work and the actual shape of the cut-outs was an asymetric curve. I found that with careful work with the needle files, this subtle shape could be created from the part supplied and with the beading added, the cab took on a completely new character. I also added the two handrails that were fitted to the roof (but which are not mentioned in the instructions) together with the spectacle rims (which are) and the cab was then ready to attach to the model.

Before fitting the cab, I took the opportunity to add a little more detail to the tank tops whilst the space was still relatively unobstructed. In particular, I added the four lifting rings. These, I have discovered, are surprisingly easy to make, using thin copper wire and a drill of suitable size. The wire is wound tightly around the drill shank several times and then the wire is cut through, laterally, with a sharp Stanley knife. This separates out a series of open loops which are then carefully rejoined into a ring with a tiny spot of solder. Bend a loop of copper wire to form the retaining bracket and the completed ring is ready to solder in place on the tank top.

At this stage I was able to complete the main bodywork by the addition of the firebox and the main fittings — chimney, dome and safety valve cover. I used the cast firebox from the kit, having ensured earlier that it fitted precisely between the new boiler and the cab front. The lost-wax castings for the chimney, dome and safety valve cover were cleaned up by mounting each in the drill chuck and lightly 'turning' off any rough spots with fine files, followed by a good polish with light-duty abrasive paper and then cotton buds with a touch of Brasso. The dome came up so well that I was even tempted for a moment to move my modelling period back to a time when these engines actually carried polished brass domes!

Boiler bands have been added and the boiler soldered to the cast smokebox. The dome has been cleaned up and has also been soldered in place.

Close-up view of the cab and the new bunker. I used the etchings provided for the cab but the cut-outs in the side-sheets need to be carefully filed to the correct shape. There is no mention of the cab roof handrails in the kit instructions, but these don't take long to add.

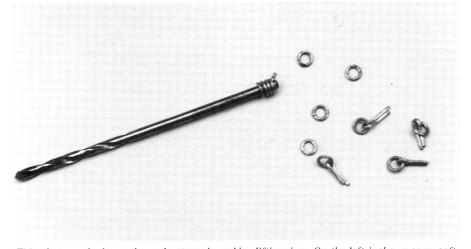

This photograph shows the main stages in making lifting rings. On the left is shown some soft copper wire wound around a suitable drill shank whilst in the centre are several rings that have been separated from the coil. Finished rings, ready for soldering into the tank top, are shown on the right.

The rear bunker has now been soldered in place and filled with Milliput to provide a base for the coal. The engine hand brake as well as the lifting rings (see previous photo) have also been added.

The addition of firebox, cab, safety valve and chimney complete the main structural elements.

Another view of the engine in the same condition as the previous photo.

The only work that remained to be done was final detailing. The fittings to the tank tops were set in place with cyano, along with the sanding boxes on the front area of the footplate. I must admit to an oversight here — most '517' class engines had sandboxes with a prominent operating arm and operating rod, both of which I forgot until after the painting stage. Remaining handrails, including the main one around the boiler and smokebox were also added at this point. It would have been helpful to have had a set of locating marks on the smokebox to show where the handrail knobs are to be fitted, but in their absence some careful measuring and marking had to be done to ensure things were straight and level. The smokebox dart provided in my kit was a bit mis-shapen but I found a better one in a spares box. I also chose to replace the cast whistles with some slightly more refined turned specimens from Springside, carefully soldered into place on the cab roof.

The kit provides quite a decent representation of the cab backhead, including one or two separate parts for regulator handles and the like. The backhead comes as a separate component, so I detailed and painted it before fitting to the finished model. Cab detailing is one of those areas where you can really go to town if you wish but I decided that what Alan Gibson had provided was quite adequate, so, with one or two exceptions, I added nothing extra. The exceptions are the two main pressure gauges which were quite prominent fittings, positioned above the firebox. These are shown on the exploded diagram that accompanies the instructions but I could find no sign of the parts in the kit. I have recently come by an old Unimat lathe and, never having touched a machine tool in my life before now, I decided that this was the time to start and that two pressure gauges were a suitable project for a beginner! So a piece of brass rod was purchased and about an hour later I had a bench covered in tiny flecks of brass and two cab gauges of which I was enormously proud — so proud, in fact, that I felt I had to show them to my wife, who couldn't believe that so much whirring of machinery had led to two such insignificant products . . .

FINISHING

The engine was now ready for the paint shops. Since after the First World War these engines were turned out in GWR unlined green and black, painting this model was not an especially difficult task. However, even on a simple painting job, it is important to prepare the ground thoroughly. So, small cracks were filled with Milliput and then carefully sanded to a smooth surface. Then the whole body was washed thoroughly in warm water with a dash of washing-up liquid and some gentle scrubbing with an old, soft toothbrush. Once dry, a light coating of self-etching primer ensures a decent surface for the main body colours.

The experts will, I'm sure, mask off different areas but I'm afraid my approach is rather more direct. The body was sprayed all over in the main colour (GWR pre-1928 green), and the black areas (footplate and valance, cab roof, tank top, smokebox and chimney) brush-painted once the primary coat has thoroughly dried — 48 hours, at least. For brush-painting I use the largest sable that I can get into the different spaces and try to let the paint flow so that it coats the surface as much through its own fluidity as through my work with the brush. In this way I find that there is less likelihood of visible brush marks remaining in the surface, once dry. Buffer beams and buffer cases were similarly treated with a matt red at the same time. The chassis had been largely painted at an earlier stage but wheels, brakes and sundry plumbing were brush-painted in matt black.

When the paint had dried hard, the etched numberplates and then the transfers for 'Great Western' were attached to the tank sides. As the photographs show, there is relatively little room for these items and it is essential when finishing a small engine like a '517' to work out positions of the letters and numbers first. It may help to draw up a tank side to scale on a piece of paper and work out exactly where each word should start and finish before you tackle the model itself.

Transfers (and, for that matter the brasswork on the numberplate) will always require protection with a coat of varnish. For engines at work, I prefer a satin finish rather than either of the extremes of a high gloss or a flat matt, so I duly sprayed a thinned coat of Railmatch satin varnish onto the body. However, as so often seems to happen to my models, the varnish didn't quite behave as I expected and left some tiny spots that were distinctly shiny. My first thought was to respray the model, but, after a little bit of experimentation, I found that the application of some of Hubert Carr's weathering powders killed the shine instead. The effect was interesting, turning the shiny areas into flat matt patches which, I persuaded myself, looked very like surface blemishes that occurred on real steam engines. So I left it all as it was. This was the first time that I had used weathering powders and I must say that I was impressed by the subtle effects that could be quite quickly built up. I also found that by working away at an area with a soft brush and just a dusting of powder produced a very natural-looking sheen on the surface — just right for an old work-horse, lovingly tended by its crew.

CONCLUSION
I am very pleased with the finished model. Okay, it isn't out of the top drawer in terms of detail and finesse, but dimensionally it is correct, has a satisfactory level of detail and, perhaps most importantly, to my eye it captures the character of the '517' class engines. Although I have been quite critical of some

aspects of the kit (and there are some cases where the design work is rather sloppy), we should remember that Alan Gibson's kit makes no claim to rival the best kits of the Finneys, Mitchells and Bradwells of this world, and it is priced accordingly. It also comes complete (except for a motor) whereas many other kits require additional purchases, especially of wheels, which further adds to costs. I should acknowledge, too, that some of the changes that I made in building the model became necessary not through design faults in the kit but through choices I made — as, for example, in the selection of a Portescap 1219 motor, which is not the manufacturer's recommended unit and for which the kit is not initially designed.

So in this light, I don't think the original kit represents bad value for money and, as I have tried to show in this article, with a little care and some extra work, we can turn what is really a basic kit into a very acceptable model engine.

The 4mm scale 517 kit from Alan Gibson, reference G4MPK19, costs £70.93 either from the Gibson stand at exhibitions or direct post free from Alan Gibson (Workshop), The Bungalow, Church Road, Lingwood, Norwich, Norfolk, NR13 4TR (01603 715862).

Compendium Crossword

Compiled by Monty Wells

The solution should appear in MRJ No. 101.

ACROSS

6 Conclusions drawn by old American trains (7)

7 Class 44 past its best (6)

8 (with *12, 30* and *35 across*, one word)
Matt substrate sometimes silencing small proprietary lines (8)

9 Insignias falsely associated with Indian Red (6)

11 Chart positive results for London (2, 4)

12 (see *8 across*)

14 Help may follow later (6)

15 Work pattern for track circuit (7)

17 Followed quad and quin but preceded deco (3)

20 The odd ace he displayed to show active service (8)

21 Now, what right does a clear starter give? (4)

22 Cliff Richard's living on top of some signal posts (4)

23 Odd to tack a rod to a wheel by this means (5, 3)

24 Start point for digitised feet (3)

28 Suggests an exact copy but railways are considerably smaller (7)

29 Flat wagon for a Baby Scot (6)

30 (see *8 across*)

32 Twelfth century market device, crossing at the platform end (6)

33 An element of fun appreciated by O S Nock (6)

35 (see *8 across*)

36 Bearing arms in non-hostile fashion (6)

37 Waters a Pacific without a driver (8)

DOWN

1 Stage show about attractive model railways (7)

2 Small Morris despatched in GWR van (4)

3 Not far off three-foot gauge (4, 2, 3, 7)

4 Recording sister of Wild Swan (7)

5 Gear for making non-stop diesel lazy (4)

7 L&NWR sweet course somewhat badly served (4, 3, 5, 4)

8 Cattle collective which had the bottle to run PO wagons (1, 1)

9 Apt way to corner (4)

10 Collect damage to left and right on the Manchester-Bury route (4, 7)

13 Relax on the way to Carlisle (6)

16 Perhaps Collett was born to it (5)

18 Could 20cwt be placed in South Wales? (6)

19 Railbus giving steady rate to track team members (5)

25 What a surgeon may do at the controls (7)

26 Dangerous obscuration which steam power contributed to (4)

27 Itch to start from nothing (7)

31 Red and white roses in railway company (1, 1)

32 Plenty of them in Left Luggage (4)

34 Valley railway of the north east twice held continental stock (4)

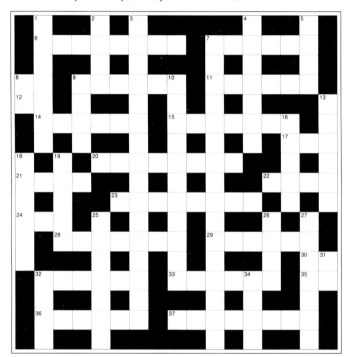

This impressive 7mm scale model of a Midland compound was built by Dave Hunt and will be described in a future MRJ.

TWO ENGINES
FROM ONE KIT

*MARTIN BLACKWELL
built a 4mm/OO Dean Goods
from a Finney kit, successfully squeezing
inside valve gear between the frames against the
better judgement of the instructions. There were so many
leftover parts for variants that he managed to cobble together a
second engine.*

The Great Western had many lovely loco-motives, but one of my favourites has always been the Dean Goods 2301 Class. These engines were designed by William Dean in 1883 and lasted up to about 1954. They were widely used on freight and cross-country passenger trains all over Great Western metals. Variations over the years included domeless boilers, fireboxes, narrow and wide running plates, altered smokeboxes and cabs and more. Tenders were generally 2500, or later 3000 gallon, but one loco did get paired with a tiny 2000 gallon tender, which I particularly like.

When the Martin Finney kit came onto the market it caught my eye, but, thinking that etched kits were beyond my capabili-ties, I did not go straight out to buy one. However, after the Guy Williams article in MRJ about the Malcolm Mitchell 44xx kit, I decided that if I could build one of these then maybe the Dean Goods would follow. So, after finishing a 44xx and taking a trip to Martin's stand at Scaleforum '94, I came away with the 4mm 2500 gallon tender kit. Due to a shortage of nickel

silver at the time, the loco followed three weeks later through the post.

My modelling has always been 4mm/OO gauge and when I looked in my showcases full of rolling stock, I was reluc-tant to change it all to EM or P4 – so OO it was. Complete wheelsets were purchased from Ultrascale at Letchworth and, once I had started the tender, the first problem became apparent. The well tank under the tender is to scale width which meant that, due to my back-to-back being 14.85mm, it would be necessary to narrow down the well tank by equal amounts both sides. Construction followed Martin's instruc-tions virtually to the letter. The castings were immaculate and the etchings perfect. I made hardwood blocks around which to form the tender body and the top flares. The corners were made good by building-up with solder and then filing back. Incidentally, I use a 60 watt SRB soldering iron with multi-core solder and a non-corrosive alcohol-based resin flux, of the type used in the aircraft industry. The only word of warning is that plenty of ventila-tion is required as the fumes are quite unpleasant! This flux literally chases the dirt from the joint and can be washed away with cellulose thinners after each session. Anyway, after all the main soldering was

done and washed up, the small castings were added using cyano. The finished, but unpainted, tender ran smoothly and accu-rately through my trackwork.

The loco kit arrived on my doorstep just as I finished the tender. My first impression was: 'Blimey, there's a lot of bits!' But once I had read through the instructions a couple of times and decided what boiler, running plate, cab, and other variants to use, things started to fall into place. The chassis instructions stated that inside motion was not possible in OO gauge but, being a glutton for punishment, I decided to have a go. I ordered the inside valve gear from Martin and, on receipt, decided that it would need some major changes to fit between OO gauge frames. I decided to take the EM frame spacers and trim them down to 12.45mm to give maximum width between the frames and to take up some of the sideplay on the wheels.

The inside cylinder block and guide-bar bracket were also milled to 12.42mm so that they slid between the frames. The front axle-boxes had to be machined away to clear the crossheads and also the centre pair to clear the crank webs and to control the sideplay. The crank axle was made from mild steel using the machine shop where I work as a CNC engineer. The following steps lay out how the crank webs and axle were made.

1. Using a 1mm grooving tool in the lathe, the crank pin was turned, thus:

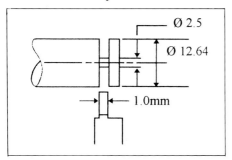

2. Held in the vice on the vertical milling machine, the stroke distance was pitched in, drilled and reamed ⅛in. The width of the web was also milled.

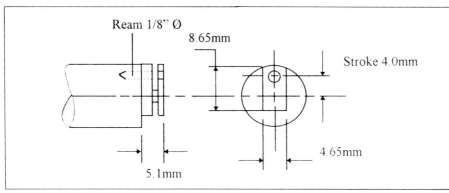

3. The crank web was parted off to a width of 2.50mm in the lathe.

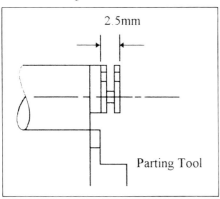

4. The crank webs were then filed to the correct shape.

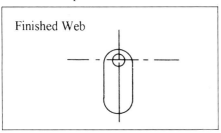

In order that the eccentrics could be put on after the crank axle was soldered together, the axle was made in the following way:

1. A length of bar was turned to ⅛in dia. from the same steel as was used for the webs and also a 1⁄16in dia. spigot was also turned.

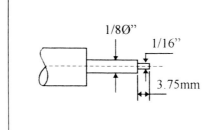

2. A second ⅛in dia. was turned, only this time it had a 1⁄16in dia. hole drilled and reamed in the end.

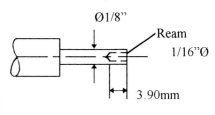

The final stage was to silver solder the crank webs in the correct place relative to the split line of the axle.

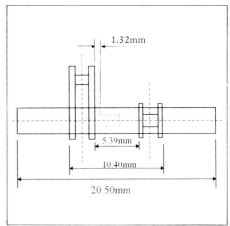

After the silver soldering, the assemblies were cleaned up and the axle was removed from between the webs using a cutting disc in a Minicraft 12 volt drill. The axle length was established at 20.50mm, then a trial-build of the eccentrics and their straps was tried. The only problem encountered was that the crank webs were hitting on the compensation beams. These were thinned down and a shim washer inserted between the axlebox and the crank web to prevent them catching.

At the other end, the marine-type little ends had to be altered as below.

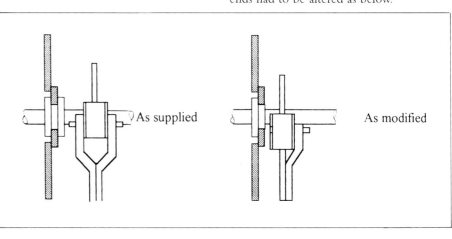

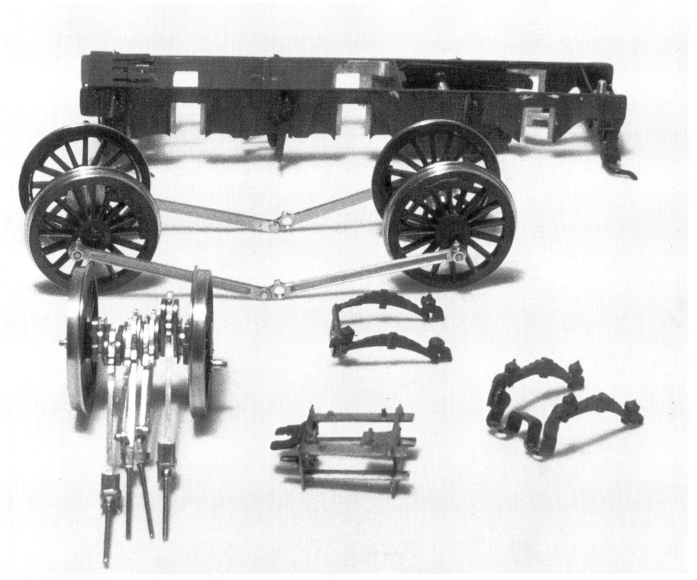

Once everything had been in and proved to be all right, the crank was built up very cleanly using the merest trace of 3-in-1 oil on the moving parts. Then, using Loctite 648 very sparingly in the ⅟₁₆in hole, the two halves were brought together and quartered by eye, not forgetting the eccentrics and their straps. The assembly was left to dry for 24 hours, after which the complete valve gear was built-up between the frames. It didn't revolve very smoothly, so a few drops of Brasso were put on the moving parts. The Minicraft drill was used to slowly run the crank assembly backwards and forwards for 10 minutes in each direction – this really freed things up and, after washing with white spirit, the valve gear ran like a Swiss watch. To retain the axle boxes the leaf springs were attached to a cross-member which was then fixed to the chassis by 10BA screws.

Crank axle assembly and cylinder block.

THE BODY

Basically, the body was built straight out of the box and to Martin's instructions. I had decided that my loco would have the later Belpaire firebox, tapered chimney, wide running plate, riveted splasher tops and cab sides and also be ATC fitted.

Starting with the running plate, no major problems were encountered but when it came to the boiler, I could not get it perfectly round at the bottom joint line, but it was close enough. I like the way all the units are dowelled together ensuring that everything remains flat to the running plate. The chimney was drilled out to produce a thin section and then, along with all the other whitemetal components, fixed on using cyano. The splasher backs could not be fitted due to my narrower gauge, but it does not show from a normal viewing angle.

When it came to the electrics I decided that I wanted to try the American system which picks up from one side on the loco and returns through the opposite side on the tender. Shorting strips on the wheels were 5 amp fuse wire in two places behind the spokes, soldered to the rims very quickly so as to avoid melting the plastic spokes. The drawbar has a phosphor-bronze wire spring connector that enables the engine and tender to be separated. The modification of the gearbox proved to be no problem and the loco ran perfectly first time. Quartering of the wheels was achieved using a home-made jig similar to that made by GW Models.

Painting was the only area I was worried about because of all the small components in the chassis. The tender axlebox bearings were masked using Plasticine as were the compensation beam pivots.

The loco chassis was taken to pieces and the wheel rims and horn guides masked with Maskol fluid. The valve gear was not painted as I thought it might interfere with the running smoothness. The loco body, tender and chassis were primed in grey. The wheels were done in black. My chosen method of painting Great Western locos is to spray the post-1938 green to get the desired depth of colour and then hand-paint the black areas using a mix of Humbrol coal black and matt black to give just the right contrast to the green. The chassis were sprayed black and then hand-painted red between the frames. Final finishing was picking out all the individual parts like vacuum pipes. Number plates were made up and fixed on and transfers applied. After a final weathering, the model was finished.

At this point I looked in the box to see all the spare parts which enable you to model other variants. Thinking it a shame to waste all those lovely etches, I decided to have a go at scratchbuilding a second loco! The tender was to be a tiny 2000 gallon which I totally scratchbuilt using Guy Williams' excellent Wild Swan book *The 4mm Engine* to guide me and Martin's construction techniques to built it up. The large water filler was the only spare part from Martin's kit.

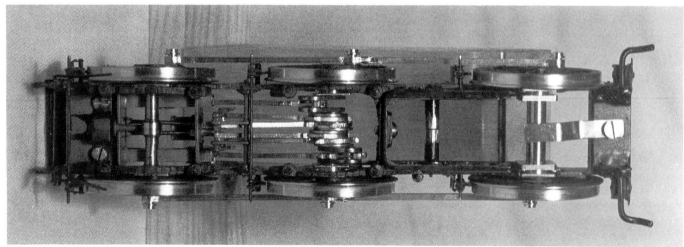

Scratchbuilt chassis assembled.

My brother's 'O' gauge Vulcan Dean Goods in the background.

The loco used narrow running plate, fluted con-rods, plain cab sides, Belpaire firebox with different wash-out plug positions, cab roof and non-ATC valance. I turned the boiler from solid brass with the boiler bands turned on and then drilled and bored out to leave a .025in wall thickness. Smokebox and firebox end plates were cut out of ¹⁄₁₆in brass plate and then soldered into position. The splashers were turned out of solid brass and then cut

across a chord to give the correct height as in Guy's book. Any riveting that needed doing was done on a home-made rivet press using different size anvils to control the spacing. All the materials used were either .005in brass for overlays or .012in nickel-silver for major frameworks. I personally think nickel-silver is a much cleaner metal to solder and would use this solely in future. The chassis was an exact copy of Martin's one and also has scratchbuilt

inside motion. This loco is going to have flange-scraper phosphor-bronze pick-ups purely because I forgot to put the shorting strips on the tender wheels.

In conclusion, I would say that Martin's kits are a pleasure to make and I am a firm believer in not wasting anything which has been so accurately made, hence the reason for the second loco! Two for the price of one – what value for money!

I recently read, in a die-cast collectors' newsletter, about the problems of creating perfect miniature vehicle body shapes, and the fact that very few manufacturers achieve it. Even when there is access to unlimited research facilities and all the dimensions are known and can be accurately scaled down, shape and styling still has to be interpreted in such a way that it has the right 'look'. So often, the subtle three-dimensional shapes of a vehicle are very distinctive and individual — a bit like a facial expression — and if not perfectly portrayed, will often fail to capture the character of the original.

The subject of this review certainly had the *look* of the prototype and a quick zap over with a scale rule confirmed that it was also dimensionally correct, so this vehicle must be rated among the few. The kit in question is one of the latest from the editor's *Classic Commercials* range and portrays one of the very familiar and characteristically-shaped Austin 'Three Way' vans. The name 'Three Way' is indicative of the three loading positions, with doors on each side and the rear, but is also, no doubt, a play on the word 'freeway'. More prosaically, Austin gave them the classification 'K8'.

The body is moulded in polyurethane resin (the now familiar Milky Bar resin) in one piece, with a second resin moulding for the cab interior. This unit comprises the floor, seats and engine cover for the front end only, and both of these mouldings were exceptionally clean and required only the very minimum of

A VAN FOR DITCHLING GREEN
GORDON GRAVETT needed a delivery van for his 7mm layout:

The body moulding after the fitting of door hinges and sprayed with grey primer.

Left: *The assembled cab interior.* Right: *The chassis is cast in whitemetal and offers an alternative style of wheel.*

The initial coat of primer was applied a little too hastily and did not take around this mudguard. The problem was remedied by degreasing with lighter fluid.

cleaning up. The chassis, wheels (there's a choice of two types of wheel centre), tyres and most of the other details are cast in whitemetal which, again, needed very little in the way of fettling. Radiator grilles (it is in three parts), windscreen surrounds, windscreen wiper and number plates are all supplied in the form of a very delicate stainless steel etch — bearing the signature of Malcolm Mitchell — to represent any chrome that may have been fitted to the van. These vehicles were available with different specifications and equipment and the amount of brightwork varies among the various photos I had to hand.

The large outward-opening doors on commercial vehicles require quite substantial hinges and on this kit, these are separate lost wax brass castings, 12 in all for the three pairs of double doors. I fitted these to the body as per the instructions but, although they were quite large on the real vans, they looked a touch over-scale on the model. I deliberated on these for some time, but comparison with photos of prototype vehicles eventually had me filing them back a bit, which unfortunately lost the cast-in hinge-pins! The basic assembly is very straightforward and once the hinges were fitted to the body, the entire assembly could be put aside for spraying. The chassis also comprised only a few components which could easily be put together within an hour or two. After assembling the chassis I rubbed it on a piece of fairly coarse abrasive paper to flatten the bottoms of the tyres — just slightly, but enough to make them look as if they were sat on the road. This had to be done very gently so as not to bend or twist the whitemetal axles.

The third assembly, the interior, was probably even quicker to make up and consisted of the floor/engine cover, two seats, a gear lever, hand-brake lever and instrument panel — which I decided to fix to the engine cover rather than to the inside of the body moulding as suggested. It just seemed easier to me to have all the interior bits as one unit that could be checked for clearance simultaneously and then painted together later.

My first move after the completion of these three units was to paint the body. I would always recommend, before any painting takes place, that the relevant parts are thoroughly degreased. With the old saying 'do as I say, not as I do' still ringing in my ears, I reached straight for the aerosol primer to give it a quick coat before going to work one morning. Most of the body covered without any problems but there was one area over the left rear mudguard which had obviously harboured some grease. Polyurethane resin mouldings often have a tendency to be a bit greasy on the surface and this often emanates from the silicone rubber moulds in which they are cast, and the problem can be even more pronounced if a release agent has been used in the moulding process. This should not put anyone off these products at all — indeed, polyurethane resin has made so many well-detailed new kits and accessories

available to us at a very reasonable cost — but it is as well to be aware of a potential problem. What I should have done before painting was to have simply wiped the surface over with some lighter fluid or switch cleaner on a cotton bud.

So, having carefully stripped all the primer off again, with cellulose thinners, and then degreased it with lighter fluid, I gave the van another very light coat of primer. The secret of painting this resin seems to be to apply a very thin coat and not be concerned about seeing the surface all covered evenly. Small spots may appear on the surface that have not

accepted the first coat properly — but be patient! After allowing it ample time to dry, another thin coat can be sprayed on, and then maybe even a third if necessary. The mistake I have made on several occasions is to try and get an even finish with the first coat — and all that happens is that if there is an area that is reluctant to accept the paint, any build-up will just run down the surface as a sag. In a similar way, if the first coat has not had ample time to dry thoroughly, a second will soften it again and the build-up of paint will also run off.

The top coat was then sprayed on, a greyish-blue in this case, and again put aside to dry out

The chassis, complete with cab and Plastikard floor.

The completed and painted chassis. The seats were given a dry-brush treatment to emphasise the padding.

thoroughly, whilst I concentrated on painting the chassis. Matt black aerosol was used as an undercoat and then Humbrol enamels for the actual colours — all shades of black on my model. The wheel centres were to represent black, but on a model I like to lighten black a little with a touch of white and in this case they were also given a hint of a sheen — but definitely not gloss. The tyres were painted a matt greyish-brown sort of colour and the chassis areas that showed a similar colour but with a little more earthy colour mixed in to represent grime.

There are some excellent 'sign written' transfers included in the kit, but the origin of two of these sets are firmly set in the West Midlands and I preferred something nearer to the South East. So, wishing to take advantage

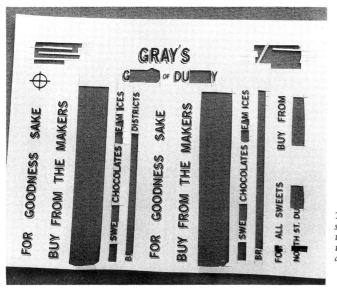

There was an ample selection of lettering on the 'Gray's of Dudley' transfer sheet to rearrange.

of the lettering, I sat down one evening with a piece of paper and a pencil and played about with anagrams of the names supplied. The 'Gray's of Dudley' set was the ideal contender and from this I made up the fictitious carpet and lino supplier, Radley's. Using a strong magnifying Optivisor and a sharp scalpel blade, I carefully cut out the individual letters required from the waterslide sheet and floated them on. The only bit of fudging required was to make extra O's using one side of a C and the other side of a D, and to make the U in 'linoleum' from two I's with some hand-painting for the loop at the bottom. Having achieved the main lettering, I then set about cutting up the small address panels for the doors and managed to give Radley's an address in Lewes.

Detailing the kit then followed as per the instructions and I particularly liked the stainless steel etched items for the distinctive radiator grille. The grille on a vehicle is like the smokebox door on a loco — it gives it an expression, and if it is not correct the model will never look convincing. This one, to my mind, is spot on and after some careful forming to match the curve at the front of the cab, fitted a treat. I laid the formed pieces on a double-sided taped scrap of plastic and carefully painted the non-bright areas cream — it seemed a great pity to cover up so much of this finely etched stainless steel, but that is the way they were. I chose the most common arrangement that I could see, and had just the three raised horizontal bars on the side portions but all the centre piece as bright.

I was a bit concerned about the paint flaking off the bright metal, so, as a precaution, I rubbed the surface over with a fibreglass brush before painting. I used Humbrol gloss, and after it was well dried I carefully scraped back the chrome strips with a sharp No. 15 scalpel blade. Fixing was with the tiniest spots of super glue, deposited off the end of a piece of thin wire, in a few strategic places.

There are also some very neat etched stainless steel number plates supplied, but being fussy, I chose to make up a set to suit the Sussex area. These were simply some white dry print letters rubbed down onto black paper and then reduced on a photocopier to the correct size. A soft pencil lead carefully rubbed over the photocopy then gave it a grey metallic look to represent the pressed aluminium plates used on most commercial vehicles at this time.

Templates are supplied on the instruction sheet to help with the cutting of the window glazing and this worked out fine, but, with hindsight, I wish I had painted the 'drop-in' recesses of the windscreen frame black, or dark grey, before fitting them, as suggested in the instructions, as the pale blue edges are a little conspicuous. A couple of 1.5mm white dots from a dry print sheet were rubbed down onto a small piece of clear transfer sheet and these

Different shades of black on the rear wheel and tyre. The body was not fixed to the chassis at the time of this photo and the wheel has slipped slightly out of line with the mudguard.

were applied to the inside of the windscreen to represent licence discs. They could, of course, have been applied to the screen before fitting — but I didn't think of them until later!

The vehicle was weathered to give it a general out-on-the-road look but was not intended to be too filthy. This was confined to some muck collected around the door hinges and in all the nooks and crannies that often get missed when vehicles are given a quick wash over but are not cleaned properly — I only had to look out to our car to get the feel for this! With the model on its side, I simply applied a drop of Humbrol thinners to the relevant areas followed by a touch of thinned 'dirt' colour so that it ran around or into the affected areas, and left it to dry out thoroughly before turning over. When all the sides were treated and dry — I like to leave paint a couple of days to dry right through — some general road grime was gently airbrushed onto the lower body sides and rear. For this subtle weathering I mix a very small amount of paint into some matt varnish and apply it as a mist, using very low air pressure, about 15–20 psi. A very gentle application is made but the effect does not show properly until it is dry so I always try not to be too heavy-handed. It is easy to apply a little more but just about impossible to take a little off!

The finished result is a model of a really distinctive and quite large postwar commercial vehicle and even if you couldn't remember what they were called, there can't be many (of my age group) who wouldn't immediately recognise the bulbous shape of the Austin K8.

A close-up of the excellent etched stainless steel components of the grille. The centre section was left bright, as were the three raised horizontal strips on the outside sections.

A GRAND DAY OUT

In the days before noses were kept pressed to the business grindstone, wafting around the railway system in an inspection saloon — complete with armchairs and kitchen — seemed a good wheeze. TIM SHACKLETON built a 4mm example to recall the day when managers were managers:

A visit from an inspection saloon was one of those once-in-a-blue-moon events that, sooner or later, seem to have happened on most lines. New works might need an official once-over; an on-site meeting might be required; or simply the powers-that-be needed an excuse for a jaunt. Through folklore and anecdote, one pictures a convivial party of technically-minded gents in search of minor problems to mull over, followed by a good lunch and then back to head office and an early finish — a far cry from the situation on today's privatised railways, where one hears that noses are kept firmly to the corporate grindstone.

Since these professional tours of inspection might well entail disembarking at all manner of junctions, sidings and civil engineering works, it is obvious that service trains were of little use for the gentlemen's purpose. To meet their needs, almost every railway provided some kind of special vehicle, often with accommodation that would not have embarrassed the company's directors and with full catering facilities on board. Most were arranged in open or saloon form and many had large side and end windows from which to inspect the passing scene. Where a view of the track ahead was important, the coach was propelled, but in the normal

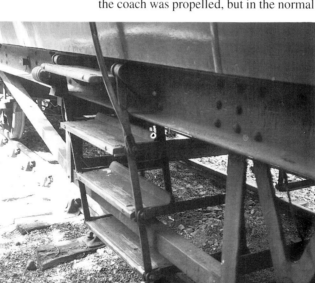

Although one or two parts appear to be missing, these close-up views identify some of the key details of the Q13 saloons.

run of events the vehicle would be hauled. In latter days, a little mogul would have been the ideal motive power but some lines kept a cherished old loco or two especially for this kind of work.

The inspection saloons used on the Western Region were typical of the breed, being purpose built to Diagram Q13 on non-standard 52ft underframes. Six of these compact-looking vehicles were produced at Swindon in 1948 to lot 1701. Numbered W80943/69/70/4/5/82, they were pure GW in design and were out-shopped in the final style of chocolate-and-cream. Perhaps because of this close affiliation with the Swindon tradition, many later carried an incorrect W suffix to their numbers. They also acquired bespoke liveries — Area Managers, Divisional Engineers and other heavies, it seem, could ride a coach and four through corporate identity schemes and have 'their' saloon painted any colour they liked.

While most of the Q13s had, by the late 1960s/early 1970s, acquired all-over rail blue or the less severe blue and grey (both with full yellow ends), W80972 was decked out in full Great Western livery while W80976 was still in the BR version of brown and cream in 1977. Later still, at least one vehicle acquired the InterCity house style. Some of these saloons travelled far from their native heath, and if the local big cheese wanted his saloon in Brecon & Merthyr livery, he could probably swing it. The last time I saw one of the very similar LMS-built saloons, bowling along the West of England main line a year or two back behind a departmental-liveried class 37, it was in gleaming crimson lake with full LMS insignia.

The sides of these saloons were quite plain but there are many subtle details — the shapes of curtains, the inner furnishings, the underfloor fittings. All go to build up character.

My inspection saloon, based on the Perseverance kit (née Westward) is equally esoteric in its choice of colour scheme. In *Model Railway Constructor* for May 1986 is a review of this same kit by Chris Leigh, which includes a photograph of W80969W in shabby carmine and cream, photographed at Edinburgh Waverley in 1967. Or at least it looks very like carmine and cream — when I checked with Chris and also with John Lewis, whose name is not entirely unknown in connection with GW coaching matters, neither was able to confirm that it definitely was in these colours or, for that matter, that it wasn't. Both, however, were agreed that there was no reason why it shouldn't have been repainted in this style, given the privileges that the great and the good granted themselves. BR abandoned carmine and cream in 1957; the latest date I have for a passenger coach still in this livery is June 1962 (better offers on a postcard, please) and at this remove there is probably no way of knowing whether W80969W was a late survivor or a one-off special.

I did as much research as I could into the painting of this particular saloon before I began construction, but came to no definite conclusions beyond the evidence of my own eyes. An equal measure of forethought is necessary in other aspects of the work, for this is quite a complicated kit to build — although I wouldn't say it was an especially difficult one. Terms such as 'easy', 'straight-forward', 'challenging' and 'nightmarish' are always subjective and much depends on the ability of the individual builder, as well as on the quality of the kit. While there certainly are some dud products out there, there is probably an equal number of modellers who would like to think they have the edge on Tony Reynalds or John Hayes but who might be better advised to stick with Big Builder. Musicians don't usually say that this or that concerto is a bunch of tosh simply because it's hard to play, but this is the way a lot of modellers seem to talk. Most good kits, like many a piano or violin piece, require a certain measure of competence but it's a brave man indeed who can admit — least of all to himself — that he simply isn't up to it.

Despite instructions that were terse and set in exceptionally tiny type — I was building from one of the earlier Westward kits, so things might have changed by now — there was nothing much to cavil over here. It's a good kit by today's standards; when it was introduced a good ten or a dozen years back, I should imagine it seemed a real cracker. It's a little out of the usual swim of things in that a lot of the fine detail that might normally not go on until quite late has, for various reasons, to be fitted rather early on; paradoxically, some of the key features of the vehicle, such as the fold-down centre steps and many of the coach-end fittings, can only be added when the model is painted.

Part location was sometimes a bit tricky, for two reasons — the absence of the fret diagram that should be mandatory for an etched kit of any complexity, and the small size of many of the components, which called for delicacy of touch and a fair turn of speed with a hot, clean iron.

There are six sets of steps to solder up and I certainly didn't get them all right first time. The roof was a bit oversize and so were a couple of interior partitions, but the other etchings were very good in terms of definition and accuracy of fit — no need here to go wading in with a big file to put things right. There's quite a decent set of underframe details in whitemetal but the castings for the interior fittings, unfortunately, were a bit lumpen and the bucket seats weren't at all the right shape and needed working on.

At this stage I got the roof finished and detailed. Most of this had to be improvised from photographs as the kit is rather sketchy in this area. Before things get too far advanced, though, some thought needs to be given to how this model is painted. The roof and underframe can look after themselves but the body is quite a performance. After priming, I sprayed the interior with a 'wood veneer' colour that owed much to Humbrol gloss tan No 9, a lovely shade that you can do a lot with in this kind of work. The interior isn't really amenable to being built up as a separate module because some of the fixtures and fittings — such as the long sofas and the folding end tables — need to be tight up against the shell of the vehicle. Before I could get cracking on these, I needed to get the outside paintwork completed. This was executed in the usual way, blocking off the windows and spraying the whole body cream to begin with. Those exterior bits that were to stay cream I masked off with 'Betto', a paper-based tape that won't stretch (unlike the vinyl type) and has sufficient tack to give nice crisp edges but not so much that it doesn't pull half the previous coat away with it. I sprayed the rest of the body carmine and then did the separate roof and underframe.

I lined the sides out with a Bob Moore pen, fitted with the fine head. The curved line under the roof at each end was a great joy and, even with a template to guide me, took several attempts. You can see straight through the big windows of this coach and so the glazing needs to be inconspicuous inside and out — there's no opportunity for sophisticated rebating here. I cut the windows out of Mylar, a strong clear film used by archivists and philatelists, just a whisper oversize and held in place with PVA. The kitchen window of the prototype is made of hammered glass and for this I used a piece of textured, translucent plastic that gives a very good match. I have had a small sheet of this stuff for

some years. I use it for lavatory windows and suchlike and for the life of me I cannot remember where I got it — probably from some kind of plastic wallet like the ones driving licences come or used to come in, only with a much finer texture.

J H Russell's *Great Western Coaches Appendix No 2* provides a couple of interior views with excellent detail of the upholstery. This was elaborately patterned but I hadn't a clue what colour it was beyond a vague intuition that it might be some kind of greyish-blue. This became something of an obstacle until, happening to be visiting a preserved railway to photograph something else entirely, I discovered a shabby-looking Q13 saloon parked up on a siding and looking very sorry for itself. The doors were locked and the curtains were drawn but there was just enough of a chink in one to enable me to discern the ratty remains of an armchair in the now-familiar fabric. I made a careful note of the colours and the following week, on a very pleasant birthday-treat jaunt to Pendon, I found another of these armchairs, in pristine condition.

As always, Pendon was inspiration on an epic scale and I went home full of enthusiasm and ideas for kitting out the interior. I used Westward's cast armchairs and divans, with the upholstery patterns painted with a OO brush in well-thinned enamels. The tables, partitions and other fittings I made myself out of Plastikard, painted in a discreet range of varnished-wood colours that, again, were based around Humbrol's tan colour. Curtains are from tissue paper, sized with PVA glue and coaxed into holding their shape; they

are a kind of dark gold colour. One saloon is empty while a group of officials — from the Dapol range — occupies the other. As Mr Barlow observed while studying the completed model, only one of them seems to be doing any work, the rest are standing around chatting and generally enjoying their corporate jolly. Briefcases, coffee cups, newspapers and ashtrays (it's amazing what you can do with a 16BA washer) are scattered around to suggest what is, in name at least, a working party.

Although my reference picture showed W80969W looking extremely woebegone, I have finished the bodywork in a very spruce condition, as it may have been a few years earlier. The underframe is, of course, the usual mix of browns and oily black patches, while the roof is a flat sooty grey. The bits in between, though, look as if they've been freshly washed down for the big day out — this effect was achieved with the aid of a 60:40 mix of gloss and satin varnishes. The completed model pleases me no end and is very much the kind of thing in which one might imagine oneself clipping along behind an elderly 4-4-0. Sunshine is streaming in through those big picture windows, interesting smells waft gently through from the kitchen and the conversation, for once, moves away from shop and office politics towards lighter topics. I could live with that, I think.

The 4mm Q13 kit is available (ref CK3) from Puffers, 96 Micklegate, York YO1 1JX (01904 635254) and costs £32.95 post free. Wheels and couplings are needed to complete.

As with an auto coach (or a DMU for that matter), the front end of an inspection saloon immediately draws the eye. Careful effort expended here will be rewarded.